BEYOND THE SILENCE

FROM THE FAR BEYOND COMES
THE COMFORTING TOUCH OF LOVE

Nan Umrigar

YogiImpressions®

YogiImpressions®

BEYOND THE SILENCE
First published in India in 2013 by
Yogi Impressions Books Pvt. Ltd.
1711, Centre 1, World Trade Centre,
Cuffe Parade, Mumbai 400 005, India.
Website: www.yogiimpressions.com

First Edition, April 2013
Third reprint, March 2016

ISBN 978-81-88479-96-2

Message from Karl

'Mum, I also have a dream ... I dream that my Baba's name go far and wide ... that the way He functions be publicised to the farthest corners of the world. I dream that all those who love Baba will always love Him whole-heartedly and completely – not because of what He can do for you – but because He is God.'

– Love, Karl

Early Acclaim

A steady procession of the most amazing, evolved souls dance through our lives. Many of them are known and treasured locally while they live. Some attract the worship of people across the world. All of them come and go as they please and while they come to change the lives of as many people as they can, they care not about the numbers... If we are lucky, we see them in the flesh. If less lucky, we hear and read about their lives from their shishyas. And we see them through their miracles which linger like perfume in the air long after they have gone.

Meher Baba is one such Guru/Avatar/Divine personage/ Krishna. It is only after his "recall" as I call it, that many, many more people have come to Him. And that fame has spread through the writing and words of his disciples. Nan Umrigar is the ideal shishya. Through her books, written with the elegance of love and humility and a childlike wonderment, she makes Meher Baba seem attainable.

Pain that seems unbearable, often leads one down a path that proves to be where we needed to go. Nan has suffered that kind of pain, and through her pain we have learnt about Meher Baba. Thousands of people have had miracles happen to them because of Nan's son, Karl. Some of these miracles are funny and whimsical – musical notes written on the frost of a window, butterflies that land at a predicted time, elephants that look at you in a strange way... All of them have one aim: to make you believe that you are not alone, you are cherished and appreciated and wanted by the universe, and if you want to access its power – it is there for you. There are universal laws, the most profound being what we call the law of Dharma – 'Do unto others as you would have them do unto you'. This is a surprisingly difficult commandment to follow, but were you to awaken to its power, you could become one of the enlightened souls that dance the Cosmic Dance.

Her books are like delicious little soufflés. They are sweet and full of fun and grace – as the universe is. The only way they can be judged is by the yearning they awaken in you to find Meher Baba, and the Meher Baba within you.

Maneka Gandhi

Smt. Maneka Gandhi, MP, Lok Sabha

'Each incident of death makes us feel helpless, numb; not knowing what to say or what to do for those who have been left behind, their lives in upheaval. Perhaps this is why Nan Umrigar's latest book, *Beyond the Silence*, remains as relevant today, as powerful a trigger to prepare us for inevitable death, as did her earlier books... all chronicle her contact with her departed son, Karl, through automatic writing, and tell us that there is life beyond death.'

– *Life Positive* Magazine, July 2013

'She sheds more light on the spiritual master Meher Baba and affords one a deeper understanding of the real meaning of and goal of life. *Beyond the Silence* is also Nan's helping hand to those who have been struck by a tragedy similar to hers. She has done this by enabling them to build a bridge across the two worlds, through her son's messages.'

– *The Herald*, Panjim, Goa, June 28, 2013

'The first two books (*Sounds of Silence* and *Listening to the Silence*) touched many people; as her life acquires deeper spiritual meaning she moves on beyond the silence. The narration moves forward (in *Beyond the Silence*) with a collection of personal, heart-touching narrations of the phenomenal experiences people from all walks of life struck by tragedy have had when they opened their hearts to the Master, entering into His ever-growing loving fold.'

– *Gomantak Times*, Panjim, Goa, June 30, 2013

'Nan Umrigar's book *Beyond the Silence* is inspirational and insightful – A wonderful read.'

– Rhea Pillai, *Celebrity*

'I just finished reading *Beyond the Silence* and as usual I went through it in one sitting from start to finish. The experiences shared by the people were so moving that many of them have remained ingrained in my heart and mind and I am sharing them with people. What I loved about *Beyond the Silence* was the simplicity of the stories which were very touching, but at the same time so educative and important that they will guide us on our journey through life in a beautiful manner.'

– Meher Castelino, *Journalist*

Contents

Appendix

Acknowledgements

I thank all those who have had the courage to tell their own stories – it is not easy to put your innermost thoughts down on paper.

I thank Firoza Bhabha for her feedback and for editing some of the chapters in the initial stages.

I especially thank Cyrus and Soumya Khambata for helping me with the writing of so many of the chapters that have all the valuable Baba information. It would not have been possible without them.

I thank Bhau Kalchuri and the Baba Trust for so readily giving me the permission for using Baba quotes and pictures.

I thank Maneka Gandhi for her lovely and heartwarming write-up in appreciation of my books.

I thank Shiv Sharma for agreeing to edit the book and making it such a pleasurable experience for me.

I thank my publisher Gautam Sachdeva and all my readers for their part in encouraging me to write this third book.

Thank You Baba, for making this book happen.

Introduction

Meherabad was in a state of shock. The residents watched helplessly as the ambulance screamed and rushed away carrying the torn and tattered bodies of two of our beloved friends, Heather and Erico Nadel, who were close disciples of Baba. They had been attacked and robbed by wandering gypsies who had camped in the vicinity of Meherabad. Erico succumbed to his injuries at the hospital while Heather battled for her life over the next few months.

As I sit here trying to make sense of this tragic event, a swarm of confusing thoughts, unwilling to accept the simple truth of *karma*, buzzes angrily in my mind. How was such a ghastly act committed within the precincts of such a holy place? Why did Baba not protect His beloved disciples? Couldn't He have taken care of them and seen them come safely through this nightmare? Shouldn't He have ensured that both Heather and Erico came out of it unscathed to live a happy life in His love and service, as they had been doing for almost the last forty years? Did they need to go through this harrowing experience? Was there a deeper meaning to all this violence that transcended our understanding?

Heather finally recovered after several complex brain surgeries, and returned to Meherabad to serve her Lord. To me, she is a living example, a monument of total faith and trust in her Master.

It made me think ... and it made me realise one thing. We are in this world for our own spiritual growth. That it is we, ourselves, who have chosen to experience certain events in our lives that will help balance out our *sanskaras*, and imbue us with the qualities of patience, tolerance, perseverance, love, gratitude, faith, and forgiveness.

It is a fact of life that no human being can grow without being tested by trying circumstances, be they physical, mental or emotional. The only choice we really have is whether to react to a situation by assuming a victim's role, or respond to it with understanding and wisdom, recognising it as a fruit of the seed we have sown in the past, and learn to go beyond.

All the Masters have experienced pain too, albeit not of their own making but to alleviate our share of suffering, and they have set an example for us to follow – so we learn how to go beyond the pain and suffering. No sincere plea for help goes unheard and the Masters are always there to help us.

Beyond the Silence explains how Baba gives us what He has to give in Silence, without saying a single word. It is in the silence of our perfect *surrender* that Baba's Silent Love flows to us. That is why this book is filled with episodes of so many people who have been struck by tragedy and difficult life situations, and how they have managed to pull through them. It is about how they have been guided and helped to grow in the most amazing ways through difficult times.

We can either choose to be rooted in pain and remain its victims or, encouraged by God's love and grace, we can make a conscious effort to overcome the suffering that our soul chose to experience in the first place.

I start here with myself ...

CHAPTER 1

My Journey Continues

January 31st Amartithi, Meherabad

This is a very special day for me as on this day our Beloved Baba dropped His human form over forty years ago, in 1969. I usually spend the day in Meherabad with thousands of others, experiencing the strength and energy that pervades the whole of Meherabad on this special day.

Around this time people from all over the country and abroad congregate on Meherabad Hill to revive and perpetuate the memory of Baba's ministry on earth and receive His blessings. To experience this phenomenon is a unique and memorable event for Baba's devotees and it becomes more so, especially as the clock moves closer to 11.45 am. That is the time when everyone begins to chant Baba's name in an increasing crescendo for fifteen minutes. After that exactly at 12 noon – 'The Silence' – is observed for fifteen minutes. It is a time when you can truly go within; merge with Baba and feel His Divinity; a time when you can internally listen to the sound of His unspoken voice and, maybe, even experience a deep spiritual fulfillment.

In the beginning when I was getting to know Him, Baba worked really hard to convince me about the splendour of this day but, having experienced it once, I made it a point to try to be there on every January 31st. However, in 2007, I could not make it to Meherabad for that day. So I did the next best thing: I gathered all my domestic help around me, switched on the computer, and shared with them the whole experience that was telecast live on the internet. We became one with all those gathered on Meherabad Hill that day. We sang the songs, said the prayers, closed our eyes and partook of the serene Silence.

Feeling nice and rejuvenated about the whole experience, I then had my lunch. Copying the rough manuscript of my book *Listening to the Silence* on a CD, I packed a bottle of red wine and some sweets for my publisher and his staff, and marched off to give them to him at his new office at World Trade Centre in Mumbai.

But, as you may have already read in the introduction of *Listening to the Silence*, I fell down those huge cement steps as I was coming down from the 18th to the 17th floor and was immediately rushed to the hospital. The doctors there told me that I had a broken femur, a fractured ankle, and also a deep, bleeding gash on my head. The bottle of wine, the sweets, the mobile, and the CD, had all remained intact!

Nothing broke – except my bones!

Over the years, I had been on blood-thinner medicines and so had to wait it out for seventy-two hours before surgery could be performed. So, I lay on my bed with my leg strung up in traction for three whole days, and the thoughts buzzing around my head during that time were not pleasant ones. All thoughts about the benefits of silence, all the inspiring messages from Karl about why things happen the way they do, all the knowledge about the laws of karma; they all seemed to have drifted far away. Pain had taken a complete hold over me. 'Why, why?' I thought, 'Why did I to have fall today of all days?'

Three days later, I was wheeled into the operation theatre for surgery. The doctor had not yet arrived and I was left alone, cold and shivering with fright, strapped to my stretcher, in the middle of that room. Although I have come a long way in my love for, and faith in, Baba, I yet cried in despair, 'Oh Baba … either You do not love me anymore, or You do not care. Which is it?'

Just then my attention was drawn to some soft music playing in the background. I listened. It sounded so familiar. It took me a while to realise that that was Baba's favourite piece of music, 'Begin the Beguine'. This particular tune had such special significance for Baba that He had requested it to be played seven times near His body when He dropped His form. Just imagine the sense of relief and gratitude I experienced then. It reaffirmed my faith that He is always with me and would take care of me! The cold room, the fear in my heart, and the feeling of being all alone vanished into thin air.

Baba had, in no uncertain terms, made me experience His Omnipresence and had reassured me. Undoubtedly, it was Baba's response to my question and my cry for help.

The surgery over, I went back home and was confined to my bed and a wheelchair for some time. On reaching home, when I checked on my pending emails, the very first email flashed a photo of Baba in a wheelchair! The second photo that came up was Baba walking with the help of crutches. These were mails sent by the Mumbai Centre and I was struck by the precise timing Baba had chosen to comfort and console me.

Accompanying these photographs was a description of Baba's accident at Satara where He had also broken His hip bone, gone through much pain, but had held a firm resolve that He would walk again without a stick. Was this a coincidence, or was Baba trying to tell me something? I made up my mind to have the same firm attitude and work towards the same goal.

Meher Baba in a wheelchair after his accident at Satara.

A metal plate and screws held the shattered bones of my femur together, and I began to live my life again as best as I could. The first two months showed that the leg was healing well but after that, although I struggled every day going miles to the hospital for physiotherapy, there seemed to be no further improvement. At the end of a year and three months, the plate and screws were beginning to loosen and the doctor decided it would be better to go in for a hip replacement. So on 9th April 2008, I was back in the hospital in the very same operation theatre and the hip replacement was done.

The leg certainly felt much better and stronger after that and very soon I was ready to walk. Back in Pune, I continued happily with my exercises, hearing encouraging accounts from other friends who had had similar problems. I was very close to achieving what Baba had inspired in me and was soon ready to attempt climbing steps once more. My physiotherapist suggested that we take one more X-ray to ensure that everything was in place, and that is what I did. The X-ray was sent directly to the doctor and I happily went to my appointment with him. The doctor put my X-ray up on the screen and a gasp escaped our lips. The light shone through the plate to show that the hip replacement shaft had pierced through the outer side of my thighbone and it was peeping through – its point clearly visible in the X-ray plate. I could scarcely believe my eyes. As for my doctor, he just kept saying, 'Oh my God … Oh my God!' In all his experience, he had never seen anything like this before.

To cut a long story short, a few months of consultations followed and then another surgery was scheduled. It was decided that we had to remove the existing shaft and put in a longer one. But there were many ifs and buts. My doctor was not prepared to put me through so much. So, it was decided to keep a bone graft handy just in case.

The surgery was scheduled, of all the days, on 4th October 2008, which was Karl's birthday. Can you believe that no other day was available? The room, the day and night nurses, the blood donors had already been arranged – all except the anaesthetist. But since I didn't know anyone, I left it to my doctor to get the best one for me. On communicating with Karl a day or two before the surgery, he assured me that he had specially chosen this day; that he would be there with me through the ordeal and that I was not to worry.

The fateful day arrived.

On the way to the hospital, we got a call to say that the occupant of the room we had booked would only be ready to move out after my surgery was over. So, on arrival we were ushered into a dismal looking, small room with no toilet attached. To top it all, another call came to say that the nurse we had booked would not be able to come. I checked into the hospital in a rather depressed frame of mind. What more awaited me? I sent up a silent plea, 'Baba, please help! Where are you, Karl?'

Just then, there was a knock on the door and a young, clean-looking man entered. He held my hand and said, 'Good evening Mrs. Umrigar, I am your anaesthetist and I am going to be with you throughout the surgery. You do not have to worry anymore because I am going to look after you through it all. I will always be at your side and if you need anything, you just have to tell me. My name is Karl – Dr. Karl Vazifdar.'

You can imagine my ecstasy! The dark and dismal hospital room turned into fairyland for me. So did the operation theatre, for Dr. Karl was as good as his word. He was there first thing in the morning to wheel me into the theatre. He sat on the right side of my head through the entire surgery; his smiling face giving me all the courage I ever needed.

Today, I still have the shaft inside of me poking its head out of my thighbone. As expected, it did not come out and a bone graft was done. They say it will take a year for the new bone to fuse with the original bone. I am back home again in Pune, not fully recovered, but definitely more comfortable and with much less pain. There is however one small drawback: although I am not confined to a wheelchair, one leg is a little weaker than the other and I have to support myself with a stick. In the beginning, this was very upsetting and I found myself wondering why I needed to go through this particularly painful period of my life. I tried to find the answers and, at times when the pain was severe, I would once more question why Baba and Karl were even allowing me to go through this.

It was then that the thought came back to me that Baba Himself had experienced intense physical pain following His second automobile accident in 1956. His head and face were badly hurt, His tongue was torn and, worst of all, His right hip was fractured and the broken bone slightly displaced. He walked with a limp for the rest of His life.

The history of past advents reveals that the leg was one part of their body that always sustained injuries. For instance, Lord Rama's leg was injured during the battle with Ravana. Lord Krishna died of injuries to His leg. And, Jesus also limped as a result of an injury to his hip. Was this Baba's way of comforting me or making me realise that if He and the past advents have gone through so much pain, why shouldn't we mortals go through the same with fortitude and courage?

I still do not know what the future holds for me. But I definitely see the incident in a better light now; that maybe it was in my destiny to fall that day, and the way I fell could have paralysed me for life. Worse, I could have even died that day. Today I really thank Baba from the bottom of my heart for always finding a way to show me when I stray, or start having doubts in my mind.

For me, it was a clear and poignant sign from Baba indicating that pain is part and parcel of one's life; that each one of us has to go through it and face our own karma boldly and move on in life. I also found myself understanding that I had possibly chosen these events for my own growth as, most certainly, they tested my patience, tolerance and reaction to unpleasant situations like pain.

What also dawned on me was that pain is inevitable, but suffering is a choice. This helped me check my remorse and greatly helped reduce my suffering, knowing that Baba too had gone through much worse. No doubt Baba's suffering is of an entirely different nature altogether as He has often said, *'People suffer for their own karma, Masters suffer for humanity, and the Avatar suffers for each and all in creation.'* Maybe Baba took away a lot of my karmic debts this way and helped me to get free. Who knows? Maybe it is a lesson for me to not only look at the past or the present, but to look at what lies beyond ...

When asked, Karl said that I had been an orthopaedic surgeon in my last life!

How Baba sent

For what I am just about to tell you, I will have to take you back a little in time to when my second surgery had just got over. As some of you may know, I was more or less confined to my home. So I took the opportunity to sit for as long as I could at my computer, in order to put finishing touches to my book *Listening to the Silence*. Most of the chapters were ready, but I still had to give it a final run-through before I sent it to the publisher for review.

I was in the middle of editing one of the most important chapters titled 'Patrick' regarding my coming across Patrick Maclane Carlson (the boy in the red shirt through whom Karl had come on my very first trip to Baba) at the *Samadhi* in Meherabad – when suddenly my cell phone rang. It was a friend from Delhi calling to tell me about a healer who seemed presently to be rocking Delhi with his prowess. 'You have to call him, Nan Aunty,' she said. 'He is very good and I'm sure he will be able to help you with your leg. I will SMS you his name and number right away.'

Not being in the best of moods, I thought, 'Forget it – what can he do for me? My hip has been replaced, and yet both the surgeries have not been too successful, so what is he going to do … make me walk?' One tends to get so cynical in the midst of pain and suffering, and that is what actually makes it all the more difficult to handle.

My cell phone beeped to indicate an incoming message. It read, 'His name is Patrick and he comes to Mumbai on every alternate Wednesday. You need to contact him, Aunty.'

I sat up with a start. That name, Patrick! The coincidence was too startling to be ignored. Here I was editing a chapter by the title and here was someone of the very same name and, that healer being recommended to me – totally out of the blue!

I dialled his number. He picked up the phone. I told him who I was; told him all about my fall and the subsequent problems I had. He answered, 'Yes, I know, I have read your book *Sounds of Silence*. My family is also connected with horses – we owned a few in Bangalore some time ago.' He then gave me details on how to get in touch with him in Mumbai and asked me to call him on a particular day. I was ecstatic and gleefully called my friend and told her about it.

'You mean you have already spoken to him, Nan Aunty? That is certainly a surprise to me, as normally he is so busy that he hardly ever picks up the phone. Usually, one has to call him for several days before one can get an answer.' The conversation ended but it left me with a funny feeling that somewhere, somehow, Baba had arranged it all for me. However, I had to wait a few months before I could go to Mumbai to meet him. I was informed that he conducted his sessions at a flat on Napean Sea Road, and off I went to meet him.

I walked in to see a very tall, thin, soft-spoken man with long hair that fell to his shoulders. He looked a little like Jesus and had a certain confidence about him that appealed to me. He listened with close attention to the details of my accidental fall, my broken bones, the surgeries etc. He closed his eyes, put his hand up near his right shoulder, and said a silent prayer, or so I thought. My meeting with him lasted only three minutes and then I was ushered out. That was it. To me, being so used to George Chapman's spirit surgery in Wales, which took at least a good half-hour, this hardly seemed to have been a healing session!

A few weeks later I went in for my third surgery at Breach Candy Hospital. Two or three days after it was over, I was surprised to see a strange face peeping into my room at the hospital. It was Patrick! Oh, was I happy to see him! On his fortnightly visit to Mumbai, he had heard that I was in hospital and had come to give me healing. I will never forget that kind gesture. In the middle of his busy schedule of seeing people, who kept waiting in a long queue outside his room, he had made time to visit and help someone in hospital! To me it was reminiscent of Baba's Grace all over again.

But it did not end there.

One day, after I was better and had moved back to Pune, I got a call. It sounded like someone's secretary was on the line. 'Dr. Patrick is coming to Pune and would like to know if he could hold a healing session at your place.' Just like that. No preliminaries, no hesitation. Patrick would be in Pune … and would be coming to my house too. It had to be Baba's Grace. I was more than thrilled!

The day arrived. The news seemed to have spread and very soon many people came over, including my neighbours who live down the lane in my complex. Dr. Patrick's healing session has now become a regular feature and, because of privacy and convenience, we have shifted the venue to the last bungalow in my lane, thanks to its kind and generous owners, the Maharaj Singhs.

Am I now convinced that just a three-minute prayer can make a difference and heal your condition? Of course! I am definitely feeling so much better and no more do I have any pain. I have a lot more energy and can even sleep the night through. However, as you may probably think, that could be because nature also heals. Or, maybe it's just blind faith. I wondered about this a great deal until I attended a three-day workshop held by Patrick. There I discovered several truths about his life and how he began to do his work for humanity. For me it was just as if Baba brought him to my doorstep, and now I place implicit trust in Patrick and his method of healing.

(Note on Patrick in Appendix D)

Due to my troublesome leg, my trips to Meherabad got terribly restricted. I was always longing to go and bow down to Baba and there were so many waiting to go with me. I know only too well how much it helps when someone is there to introduce and show you around during one's first visit and, although the receptionists there are always kind and generous with their time, I have always made it a point to try my best to be there with newcomers and to show them the various aspects of this incredibly peaceful haven called Meherabad.

Now that this was not possible, I was in a bit of a sulk. I guess the ego also has a way of playing its role at such times and I wondered how newcomers could possibly feel welcome and looked after if I was not with them. And suddenly, like a bolt from the blue, almost in response to my thoughts, I get a call from a young boy called Yohann Noble to inform me that now he was on the Welcome Committee at Meherabad and would gladly help escort any newcomers that I would like to pass on to him. You cannot imagine the relief and gratitude I felt. How lovely to have someone waiting there, on call, to help you with the bookings, to show you to your room and to point out all the important spots and salient features of Baba's life and work.

I have now made this into a regular feature and just so that you know who he is – here is his own story of how he came to Baba and how happy he is there.

Yohann Noble

My name is Yohann Noble and I was born a dyslexic child. Being totally ignorant about the problem, I suffered agonising days when I was in school. Besides doing badly in studies, I used to get beaten by the teachers quite often for small things or, sometimes, even for nothing at all. As I grew up, I was plagued with questions: 'Why was I suffering so much?' 'What had I done to deserve this?' 'Why did these terrible things happen to me, especially when I was always trying to do the right thing all the time?'

I struggled to get through each moment, each day, and each year. It was not easy because I never got a chance to do anything I liked. I loved to take part in sports, theatre, hobby classes, athletic training, scouting, but nothing worked out, as I always had to spend most of my time just studying. Consequently I became a very quiet and shy person and, because of this, I was either at home all the time or just going for tuitions.

Then at last, my Tenth Standard Board Exam was over and for the first time in my life there was no more studying to be done. My life changed. Being an introvert, I had made no friends and had cultivated no interests to occupy my time. This intense loneliness made me ask myself some of the most important questions of my life and that slowly began to sow the seeds of enlightenment.

But a strange thing had happened a couple of months before the exams had even started. I had seen a white book on my mother's bedside table. Browsing around in her room one day, I saw this book again and asked her what it was all about. Mom told me to read it, saying, 'You may like it.' So I took it to my room and looked at the cover. It read *Laws of the Spirit World – Vol. 1.*

The introduction spoke about an incident that took place with a Parsee couple, Mr. and Mrs. Bhavnagri, who had lost their two boys in a car accident. I read far into the night, up to the stage where the two boys began communicating with their parents. The stories I read answered many of the questions I had asked myself during my agonising school days.

I woke up the next morning, a completely changed human being.

Each night, the more I read, the more it helped to change my way of thinking. It revolutionised my approach towards life. I then went on to learn *Reiki*, as it was the popular thing in the mid-90s. At the Reiki class there was a middle-aged Parsee lady who happened to mention the name of Meher Baba and said that she dreamt about Him very often. When I heard the name Meher Baba, it rang a bell in my subconscious. I wondered who was this man and why I was feeling this curious pull towards finding out more about Him.

I now started reading books on spiritual subjects and found many of my questions being answered. But then, many more questions came up. I also needed answers to these questions. Where was all this leading me, and where would it end?

Amongst this question-answer frenzy, I asked Mom if she knew who Meher Baba was. She said, 'Yes, don't you know? He is that Irani man with long hair.' Then one day she brought home this book called *Sounds of Silence* and told me, 'Yohann, you were asking me about Meher Baba the other day, so I picked up this book for you, it has something to do with Him.' I was extremely moved by the reality of *Sounds of Silence,* and more so because it touched upon the two subjects that were closest to my heart – the Bhavnagris and Meher Baba. I read the initial pages again and again, reliving all that the mother had gone through. I marvelled at how Meher Baba had reached out through her dead son to make Himself known to the family.

Although I was just half-way through, I became so engrossed in the story that I had failed to realise that for the past couple of months my parents had been disappearing from the house on Saturday evenings. When I asked them about it, they gave me vague answers. When I persisted, they told me that they go to this séance session at Girton High School.

I said that I wanted to come as well. At first they said, 'No,' but finally they agreed and I went along with them. I was interviewed by the group's leader who was called Tara and we had a small discussion. Around 6 pm an old couple and some more people came in. Mom told me the couple were mediums known as Mr. and Mrs. Kapadia.

Mrs. Kapadia soon went into a trance. I was specifically told by the leader not to get up but, to my surprise, the first thing the spirit guide (Mother Catherine) did was to point at me and ask me to stand up. In my simple way I understood that this is a higher authority asking me to do something, so I obeyed. Mother Catherine spoke to me and told me one important thing: 'There are many roads to God and you must choose one.' I kind of grasped what she was saying and, even without knowing much about Meher Baba, I understood that here was a definite command and I must follow it.

I finished *Sounds of Silence* and came to a decision. I would make a trip to Meherabad. We went there on 30th January, which was just a day before the Amarthithi (Baba's Death Anniversary). After taking *darshan*, I noticed there was a bookstall close by. Since I was keen on reading a book written by Meher Baba Himself, I asked the person to give me a book that Baba Himself had written. He showed me *Discourses* and I bought it.

When I started reading it, I was totally amazed. Not only had Baba answered all my questions that had been left unanswered for so long but He had also given me more knowledge about things I had previously not known. At last, I was satisfied and realised Meher Baba is no ordinary Saint or Master. He is beyond that.

By this time I was already in college. Things were still difficult but the difference was that before this I did not know how to live my life. Now with Baba, I was happy and content. But when it came to socialising, I suffered a lot and struggled to make friends. I was still a loner and would go for outings and movies alone. The only place I got to meet more people was in Meherabad. Somehow, with Baba's help, I seemed to get along well with everyone there. In Meherabad, Baba seemed to allow me to socialise and make friends, but once I came back to Mumbai I was back to square one and my best friends continued to be my computer games, books, movies and music.

So I began visiting Meherabad more often. I really loved staying there and being close to Baba. That continued till one day a strange thought entered my head. What if I really stayed here and began to do some work for Baba? But I still had some responsibilities I needed to fulfil, like helping with the family, getting married and settling down. So I started working in a hotel instead and then, later, in a Human Resources firm.

As usual, I was doing quite badly and my boss wanted to fire me. He called me into his cabin and told me frankly that although they were happy with my conduct and discipline, my performance was unsatisfactory. He said I would be put on notice period for one month and, if my performance improved, then he would reconsider. I agreed to that as it seemed fair enough.

I continued to work and a month passed. I did not realise it but there was a remarkable improvement in my performance. Instead of throwing me out my boss gave me an increment. I was now even training others! This continued for a year, till I knew for certain that yes, this is it – now is the time to go and work in Meherabad.

I did not tell anyone at home. I quit my job. I told my parents I was going to Meherabad for an extended period. I knew they would not at first be too comfortable for me to shift there, but finally they accepted my decision.

I am now working in Meherabad full time in the Welcome and Information Office. This office was set up to help new people when they walk in for the first time. Baba had put me where I belonged.

I constantly get calls from people wanting to know more about Baba: how He lived, what He did, and what He said. I spend my days in happy contemplation of how Baba has turned my life around from being a recluse, to meeting so many new people. I enjoy taking people around, and talking to them about Baba.

Now when I think back to the early days, the days when I used to go for the séance at the Saturday meetings, I remember that at one point, Mother Catharine had clearly told me, 'Whether you like it or not, you will be doing God's work.'

(Yohann can be contacted on yohann.noble@ambppct.org)

Cyrus Khambata and I met a long time ago. It was sometime during 1986-87, when I was still living in my old home at Eden Hall, Mumbai, that I had called him up to ask if he could recommend some books on Baba to me. I remember him riding up on his scooter with the sidecar filled with Baba books. I think Baba sent him into my life to give the added push I needed, and that still persists till today.

When I was writing *Sounds of Silence*, he helped me by not only giving me all the necessary literature on Baba, but also by relating to me in his own special way, all the little anecdotes he knew about Baba and His life. There was a gap of about two years in which I did not meet him, but our friendship was renewed after I had moved to Pune, and yet used to spend a few months each year in Mumbai at the Cricket Club of India. He has remained a dear friend to me and never fails to enlighten me with his vast knowledge about Meher Baba. My second book *Listening to the Silence*, as well as this one, has a lot of inputs from him and his wife Soumya.

Our Beloved Avatar Meher Baba has placed Cyrus at His Bombay Centre as the person responsible for conducting the Tuesday Study Circle on 'Baba's Words' given by Him in His *Discourses, God Speaks, Beams, The Everything and the Nothing* and other such books. The resulting discussions have provided a platform for understanding the how's and why's of life with insights on making appropriate choices to handle diverse situations of life in the light of Baba's messages. The on-going process of learning and growth as a result of the discussions and shared experiences have enabled Baba lovers, including Cyrus, to enrich themselves by making their lives more impactful and the journey of life more joyous. Besides the Study Circle, Cyrus also helps in conducting the Thursday Open Forum, which is formatted to share Baba lovers' testimonies of His love in their lives, and sharing of news and activities in the Baba community.

How does Cyrus know so much? I will now let Cyrus tell you how, being a young descendant of a priestly and religious orthodox family, he learnt to love Baba and has stayed on to be such a fine example to humanity.

Cyrus Khambata

How did I come to be placed at the Centre? Well, it was a series of well-defined situations that brought me into Baba's fold. Being born into a *Zoroastrian* priestly clan, my family was into orthodoxy and did not believe that there could be anything superior to Zoroastrianism. Babas, *Swamis, Gurus,* were a far cry from it. I was a regular at the *Agiary* (*Parsi* fire temple) from an early age, always beseeching this Supreme One, *Ahuramazda,* to reveal Himself, if He did exist, and to show me a way to find Him.

As the years rolled by, my interest turned to reading life stories of saintly persons belonging to other religions as well. I started buying the *Thus Spake* series of booklets. My favourites were Sri Ramakrishna Paramhamsa and Swami Nityananda. The transformation from a narrow religious approach to a more broad-minded one thus occurred.

One day in October 1968, at my friend Jimmy Patel's home, a discussion arose about Meher Baba. The episode of how Meher Baba came to the rescue of a person, who was constantly abusing and spreading negative propaganda about Him, touched a deep chord in my heart. It showed Baba's magnanimity, forgiveness and mercy. Further enquiries about Meher Baba revealed that Baba claimed Himself to be God in human form, the same one as Zarathustra, Rama, Krishna, Buddha, Jesus and Mohammad. I wondered if this was in response to my persistent yearning for an answer from Ahuramazda?

I sought further information and was promptly lent the book *The Perfect Master* by Charles B. Purdom. The author begins his book with ... 'This will be found a strange book ... It is the story of a man whose life will appear incomprehensible, a life in which the contradictions of normal values and actions are prominent. Yet this man says, 'I am God,' and His mission is to change the world, though He neither speaks, nor writes nor even seeks to get followers. It will arouse controversy, and I have no doubts that it will be misunderstood ...'

What an honest and powerful way this was to begin the book, I thought to myself. The author leaves the decision on the reader to believe in Baba's claim or to discard it. I had to find the truth for myself.

15

Back home, my newfound interest in Baba did not find favour with the family. In fact, my friend's family was squarely blamed for leading me 'astray'. As I read through the book, I saw two clear options opening up before me: one, that Baba is indeed what He says He is, God in human form. Or, two, He is a genius manipulator. I thought the only way to find that out was to put Him through a series of tests. While the tests were various and varied, these two stand out in my memory in the process of my anchoring on to Him.

Once, while in the fire temple, I observed the fire in the sanctum sanctorum in embers. I thought that if by the time I bow and lift my head instantly, I see the embers turn to flames, I would believe that Meher Baba is indeed Zarathustra come again. It happened, and what a flame arose! Yet another time, while at home, I was reciting our Parsi prayers on the balcony. Closing my eyes, I sincerely asked Ahuramazda to show me one unmistakable sign to confirm His endorsement of what I was venturing into and that Meher Baba is in fact the Advent of our times. I opened my eyes and, lo and behold! I witnessed the most spectacular sight ever. I saw a huge ball of fire glide past on the horizon. That unique and majestic sight put to rest my concern about Baba being God in human form.

During this entire process, I could feel Baba gently and patiently, without in the least condemning me, or my ways of testing Him, paving His way into my heart. It was through one of these tests that He led me to the Avatar Meher Baba Bombay Centre at Lamington Road, opposite Minerva Theatre.

Intellectually at least, I was now convinced about Baba's Omniscience and there arose in me a burning desire to meet Him. My daily visit to the Agiary was now replaced by my visit to the Baba Centre, meeting people, reading books, and gathering information. On the Centre's notice board was a circular from Baba informing His lovers about His recent seclusion, the pressure of His universal spiritual work, and a strict warning not to visit Him or even write to Him. How was I to fulfil my ardent desire to meet Him? I justified to myself that those instructions did not apply to me, as I was not yet His disciple. Keeping the whole plan a secret, I bought a train ticket for the next day and on the pretext of going for a scout's camp, I left my home – all set to meet Baba.

However, I felt a strong pull within me to first go to the Centre and take Baba's darshan before proceeding on the train journey. By this time, I was already fine-tuned to such intuitive voices and I felt this was Baba's ploy to stall my visit. Yet, I was determined to go, come what may. As I bowed down before Baba's photo at the Centre, I heard this deep, unmistakable voice asking me to carefully go through the circular one more time. My doubts were confirmed. Baba was in fact dissuading me from going to Him. The voice was so strong and clear that I found my feet moving me towards the notice board. As I was fully conversant with the contents of the circular, having read it many times before, I went through it this time very casually, but when I came to the end and read 'Adi K. Irani, King's Road, Ahmednagar,' something like an electric current ran down my spine. I quickly pulled out the train ticket; it read 'Ahmedabad'. I was stupefied. I couldn't fathom the gravity of my blunder. The sheer beauty with which Baba spared me the arduous and futile journey, through a series of well-orchestrated intuitions, reinforced my faith in His Godhood. I simultaneously felt comforted that His benevolent *nazar* was on me.

However, instead of pacifying me, this incident now created a still greater desire – to leave home and be with Him and serve Him. After much internal deliberation, and relying heavily on His forgiveness for disobeying His order, I finally wrote to Baba in November 1968, introducing myself and asking Him to accept me as His disciple and allow me to stay with Him forever. I was then just seventeen years old, and all this was done secretly without the knowledge of my family or anyone at the Centre.

I got a prompt reply through Baba's close disciple Eruch, which is reproduced here in part:

'My dear Cyrus,

In spite of restrictions on correspondence, Beloved Avatar Meher Baba heard your very loving letter, and He directs me to inform you that He wants you to live with your family and lead an honest and pure life and not neglect your studies. He wants you to remember Him wholeheartedly and as often as you can in the midst of your daily activities! Avatar Meher Baba wants you not to commit any sort of lustful action as long as you are not married. He wants you to lead a pure life. He wants you to face the world kindly and bravely, and shoulder the responsibility that might have to be shouldered later on in your life. He sends you His Love and Blessing, and wants you to remain happy in the knowledge that those who love Him are dear to Him and close to Him ...'

That Beloved Baba actually heard my letter and took the trouble to dictate a reply, in spite of His failing health and being in strict seclusion, overwhelmed me and sealed my fate with Him forever. There was no looking back now.

Since then, my life's journey has never been alone. Baba has been my constant companion at each and every twist and turn of my life. With Baba's companionship, I feel I have been able to realign my priorities, get a sense of direction in my life, achieve a deeper understanding of why things happen the way they do, recognise the choices available to me in the moment to face up to the destiny that I have created through my own past karma, and handle the situation in the light of 'what would please Baba'. My goal is to remember Baba when I breathe my last, and I beseech Him to grant me this boon.

My observation over the last many years of conducting the Tuesday and Thursday meetings has been that the majority of newcomers who turn up at the Bombay Centre do so after reading Nan's book *Sounds of Silence*. The testimonies that we get to hear about their coming to Baba are so intriguing, that one cannot but marvel at the unfathomable ways Baba uses to bring each lovely soul into the orbit of His love. Their having reached Baba's *Darbar*, my role with these newcomers has been to help them focus all their love and attention on Baba alone because, finally, it is love that matters; Baba that matters.

Let us all pray to our Beloved Avatar Meher Baba to help us grow in His love and lead a life that will glorify and please Him.

(Cyrus can be contacted on mehercy@gmail.com)

CHAPTER 3

Baba's Grace

After my accident, various complications after the surgery on my hip ensured that I spent a large part of the day confined at home. Despite this, I tried my best to just get on with my life. It struck me that we are all made to go through certain rest phases in our life, which are really our dull days. Many spiritual books mention that these are the times when we are to actually stop 'learning' and need to put into practice the truths we have been taught. It is during these dull days that one has time to introspect, look at one's life, identify faults and deal with them in a calm and peaceful manner. The hustle and bustle of a normal day seldom allows for this. However, I have to admit that I really missed my visits to Baba's Samadhi.

So after three long years, on 16th January 2010, my daughter Tina and her husband Pesi decided it was time I went to Meherabad again, but thought that, perhaps, I was too hesitant to ask. So they called to say they had arranged to go for the day and did I want to join them? Of course I did!

As usual, Karl was thrilled … His message that morning said he was very happy that we would be coming and that he would be a smiling face to greet us when we reached there.

So, we packed a few sandwiches and set off from Pune at midday and reached Meherabad by around 3 pm. From the car park to the Samadhi is a short walk on a rather uneven surface. Because of my troublesome leg, I was concentrating so much on walking over the gravel that when I looked back, I was surprised to see someone hugging Tina and Pesi. I got a glimpse of blue eyes under a bright red cap complementing a red shirt and brown pants – colours reminiscent of Karl's first spirit appearance at the Samadhi long ago. As soon as the man saw me, he rushed towards me. Smiling broadly, he put his arms around me and hugged me tight. I was thrilled. The next thing I felt was his body shaking with uncontrollable sobs. My goodness, I wondered. Who was this? What had suddenly happened to the smiling face, and why was he crying so much? When he managed to get a hold over himself and raised his head, it was my turn to get the shock of my life. 'Oh, my God!' I cried. 'Can it really be you? After so many years, and of all places here at Meher Baba's Samadhi!'

He ushered me into the Tomb area assuring me that he would wait for me till I had taken darshan and come out again. He was as good as his word and we sat down to talk.

Who was he and why had I got such a shock?

Merwan Masters

It was Merwan, a very close relative of mine who had loved Karl dearly. He was not a horse-lover but used to come to the races with us only because of Karl. We had spent many happy days together and he had been really devastated when Karl passed away.

Years passed by, and when *Sounds of Silence* was finally published I had gifted him a copy but he never read it. He was what we call a 'Mad Parsi' and a devout follower of Zoroaster, who would visit the Agiary almost every day. Therefore, Meher Baba had no meaning for him. To add to this, he had unfortunately drifted away from the family and, during the last twenty years, had started living in a farmhouse far away from civilisation. He was upset that his daughter had married a non-Parsi and, even though he loved her dearly, he had broken off all communication with them, so much so that even when the grandchildren were born, he stayed away. The last time I had seen him was briefly at my husband Jimmy's funeral in 2007, when he had come just to pay his respects. So you can imagine the shock I got when I saw him at the Samadhi that day. But the shock was even more intense when he told me how he had come and why he was there.

Merwan said, 'I was cleaning out my old house when I came upon your book *Sounds of Silence*, still in its original wrapping. For lack of anything else to do, I opened it and read it. Memories of Karl overcame me and on an impulse I decided to see what this Meher

Baba was all about. So I said to Him, 'See, Meher Baba, I am just visiting your Samadhi and have not come to take Your darshan or touch my head down on Your tombstone, because I do not believe in You, nor am I likely ever to do so. I am only coming to see what You are all about. Not a single soul knows that I am here except You and me, and so I am putting You to the test and want You to prove Yourself. I want to know if and how Nanny will come to know that I was here. This is what I said to Baba, so now can you imagine my reaction when you actually walked in? I just could not believe my eyes when I saw you get out of that car ... I thought, was that really you? And that is why I cried so much. You know, somehow in my heart I kind of had a feeling that something was going to happen, but this ... this is too, too much! For not only did you come to know about it, but Baba actually brought you before me in person. It's not as if I was here for the whole day, not even for an hour, but just for ten minutes, and I am still finding it so hard to believe that just during those ten minutes – you walked in!' And he continued to sob his heart out.

'Dear Merwan,' I said, 'I have also come today after almost three years and am here just for a few minutes to bow my head and touch it to the Samadhi.'

So, instead of just a few minutes, we spent the next couple of hours together. Baba made sure that Merwan saw everything, and I even took him for tea to the Pilgrim Retreat. The receptionist took one look at his fair skin, his blue eyes, the red cap on his head, and burst out, 'My goodness, you look like Paul Newman!' And by that time, just like Karl had said, his face was smiling broadly again.

I don't know if he will ever visit again, but I have a funny feeling that this story has not ended.

———————

The story I just told you was written by me in early 2010, but I have to continue it now for that funny feeling didn't fail me. In 2011, I got a call to say that Merwan had taken ill and been admitted in a critical condition at a hospital in Mumbai. I made it a point to go visit him, and found him looking very weak and frail. When he saw me he opened his eyes, smiled and asked, 'Meherabad?' I assured him that I had just been there and would pray for his recovery. He pointed to himself and gestured, 'Me too ... six times ... on a motor bike.' I could not help smiling to myself, 'Oh my goodness, how Baba works!'

But there was more to come.

A couple of months later I got the news that Merwan had passed away. I went to his funeral and sat through the prayers, with so many thoughts whirling in my head. After it was over, his sister came up to me and said, 'Nan, may I have a moment? You probably have no idea how my brother's life had changed after reading your book. He was often very short-tempered and rude whenever he was here, but then his whole attitude seemed to change to one of kindness and love and do you know he even brought me a box of *mithai*. But more than that, will you believe me when I tell you that he even made his way back to his home with his wife, actually called for his non-Parsi son-in-law, spoke to his children, spent time with his grandchildren and then, as if his work was kind of completed, he passed away in peace. Nan, can you please also take me to Meherabad?'

I left there with many thoughts about Baba's wondrous ways whirling in my head.

But wait! I'm not done, because there was still more to come.

When the family went to his farmhouse to clean it, they found that it was full of Meher Baba books and Baba's face smiling down from every wall! Now, wouldn't you call this a miracle?

Jimmy Umrigar

Decisions by the family to go to Meherabad were always greeted by me with the greatest of pleasure and anticipation. So, when Sabita suggested, on 25th July 2009, that all of us go together just for a day, it meant that a lot of organising had to be done. But by the end of it, only the five ladies of the family made the short trip.

Although by now Meher Baba was the prime focus of our attention, nothing was ever complete without first having a conversation with Karl the day before. But this time, my discussions with Karl were more about the fact that in all the nine years my husband Jimmy had been with Baba, he had not made any effort to ever make his presence known to us. 'Where is he Karl? Yes, I know that he is well, he is happy, and sometimes he does come to talk, but in all this time I am sure he has made some kind of spiritual progress with Baba. Can he not also show himself to us at least once?'

And this is what Karl replied ...

'Singing in the rain and being with you in the rain, is what it will be; many of us singing together in the rain, and you also with us; me in the centre, Dad by my side and a lot of people around us. But I am the voice. I am the singer and the song, and Dad my accompanist. You may have a greater vision of him because he is big and strong, and I am the smaller and weaker one, but with the voice of a singer of repute. I am the singer, and Dad is with me. Hope we shall make music together, Mum.

Love you lots ... Karl'

'Oops, at last!' was my reaction. 'This is something I have to see!'

The journey was smooth, the day cloudy, and the sky overcast. It was cool, but windy. At this time of the year, the Pilgrim Retreat had few visitors so there was plenty of space and opportunity to wander about at will; to be alone with your thoughts. Each of us spent time with Baba at the Samadhi the way we wanted; kneeling at his tomb, or just sitting around. While some of us spent a few moments in Baba's room, others just wandered under the trees, looking up at the beautiful sky, and just listening to the silence.

But where, I wondered, was the 'singing in the rain' that Karl had talked about? Not much chance of that I thought! Yes, it was drizzling but since it was mid-morning there was no chance of an *aarti*, and even less chances of any kind of music at such a time. Knowing well Jimmy's nature, we all went along with the flow and made our way back, in time for lunch, to the Pilgrim Retreat.

However, on our way out from the dining room, we came across a young man carrying a guitar. Oh, I thought ... here is a musician ... but it was just a passing thought until my eyes fell on a notice posted on the board, which said that there was going to be a concert that evening at the old Pilgrim Centre where a reputed guitarist would be playing. Our curiosity was aroused and we decided that we should drop in there on our way home in the evening.

By that time it had started raining heavily, and the concert had already begun when we walked in. Yes, there was the same young boy I had bumped into a while back, now seated on a small stage, with three others beside him. He was singing and the others were accompanying him. One was shaking a tambourine while the other two were strumming their guitars.

Was one of them Jimmy? And, if so, which one?

The songs were beautiful; the young boy's voice melodious. We enjoyed a lovely half-hour with them. It came to an end and we were just about to leave, when the boy looked into the audience and said loudly and pointedly: 'Dad, Dad ... why don't you come on stage and join me? Come on, Dad ... get up, come and sing with me.'

We stood rooted to the spot as we heard the audience echo, 'Yes, where is Dad? Come on Dad!' they shouted. Their cheers helped encourage a smiling, elderly gentleman to get up from the last row and walk towards the stage. He was big and strong, and we had a clear view of him as he climbed on to the stage and sat next to his son. He took up his guitar and the two of them began playing together.

Can you imagine our joy? The family could not have got a better sign, knowing how much we all loved and missed Jimmy. Baba had put my heart at rest.

Thank you Baba!

Delhi Launch of 'Listening to the Silence'

Listening to the Silence had already been launched in Mumbai and Pune and now it was time for its launch in Delhi. How was I going

Launch of 'Listening to the Silence' in Mumbai.

to manage to be there with my weak leg? I was not able to climb any steps or walk distances as one has to at New Delhi airport. That meant I would have to use the wheelchair and that really made me squirm! Though my family and friends went out of their way to make it easy, I felt really uncomfortable and unhappy at having to be wheeled along while everyone else walked. It was a real effort for me to manoeuvre both the airports, and then to get through those next few days without all the time feeling beholden to everyone around me.

After that I really did not have much time to think for there was much to do. Programmes had to be arranged, practices put in, music to be organised and a hundred other details to be looked into. Would I be up to it?

By Baba's Grace the launch went off beautifully. The venue could not have been more appropriate; the ambience more perfect. The room was beautifully arranged, the chairs clean and white, and the stage in the right position for the visuals to be screened. The flowers were fresh and green; the lighting perfect. All the speeches were meaningful; the Baba videos a revelation, and the music and songs emotionally stirring … We had people from all walks of life crowding the room to share in Baba's Love, who later stayed on to partake of the refreshments so kindly organised by the sponsors and those in charge.

It was with deep gratitude that I left Delhi airport the next day. Although I still had to use the wheelchair, it did not bother me so much this time. I landed at Mumbai airport and as we all entered the lift to go down to the luggage area, one of my friends caught my hand in a tight grip. 'Stop … stop!' she cried. 'Just look … look up!' For over our heads, there was a huge billboard that read 'Karl Umrigar Welcomes You' written in big letters and a picture of Karl on horseback smiling down at us!

I was not only amazed; I was stunned! I felt so small that tears trickled down my eyes. Why had I been so petty and upset about going in a wheelchair? What was there to feel so self-conscious about, especially when Baba was so magnanimous that He had organised such a big billboard for us in appreciation of something that we too had enjoyed so much?

You may well wonder how this billboard happened to be up there at that time. The Royal Western India Turf Club organises a

Cup race every year in Karl's memory. This year it was to be held on 27th March, and this year the Tata Group had come forward to co-sponsor it. As the event was drawing near, this was their way of advertising it and, I guess, it was Karl's way of showing himself to us.

But how amazing! How absolutely mind-blowing, that we should have been at the airport on that exact day, and walked under that particular doorway.

I thought this was a wonderful way for Baba to say thank you to us!

CHAPTER 4

The New Generation

Whenever people are asked to describe their feelings on going to Baba and Meherabad, so many of them say the exact same thing, 'Oh, it feels like coming home.' How is it that every time you go, you feel that warm golden glow, that feeling of love and security, which makes you feel protected and loved; that helps you to carry on with life, no matter the odds?

Why is the hill so green, the sky so blue, the clouds so white and fleecy? Why are the leaves so fresh and the flowers so bright? Why are the prayers so soothing, the air so light? Why do you feel like resting your head in Baba's lap and going to sleep?

Because this is where Baba lived, breathed, ate, and slept. These are the paths He walked, and the surrounding environs He was connected with. This is where He gave His darshan, His blessings, and this is the place of the Samadhi where His physical body lies. This is where His powerful energy still glows.

This is Meherabad ... Baba's resting place.

You will be surprised how many people have grown up knowing about Baba, and yet never really knowing Him; whose elders have had strong connections with Him, or who have had close family and friends connected with Him; even lived close to His home in Pune, and yet never really experienced His majesty and love. And yet it is amazing how Baba has reached out to them in different ways.

You might like to read what Yasmin Damania has to say ...

Yasmin Damania

In October 1989, I visited Meherabad and Ahmednagar for the first time with my soon-to-be-husband Jehangir, and his father Homi Damania. Their family belonged to Ahmednagar, and my would-be father-in-law had been close to Baba and His *Mandali* for quite some time.

Up on the hill, while others visited the Samadhi, I just strolled around until I got a sudden urge to sit on the platform under the sheltered portion just outside the Samadhi. I had never meditated before, but I sat there with my eyes closed. One of Mansari's (one of the early members of Baba's women Mandali and caretaker of Baba's Samadhi) fierce, snapping dogs, sensing my mood, quietly snuggled up to me.

The turning point in my life came in 1995, which proved to be a landmark year for me. Certain events of the previous year had left me very disturbed. After much internal debate and turmoil, I concluded that I needed to seek answers through stilling my mind and calming myself. Hence, in February of the same year, I joined a meditation class. That day began my journey of self-exploration and self-discovery. A few months later, an intense longing to 'heal' saw me pass through Reiki Part 1 and 2 workshops.

One day in late 1995, my husband Jehangir, while clearing out the loft, came across three books on Meher Baba, which had been lying there all this while, unread by me. He suggested that I go through them, as with my newly found interest in meditation and spiritual inclination, I might find them interesting. These books were *Showers of Grace, The Answers* and *The Everything and The Nothing*. A few nights later as I sat up in bed reading them, I had an amazing dream. I saw this picture, like a photograph in black and white, of three male figures standing at the fork of a road, with a Banyan tree's roots hanging as a backdrop. One of the men was a middle-aged person called Eruch; the other was perhaps my father-in-law, who was not living by then. I think the third was Meher Baba, who appeared somewhat hazy in the background.

A voice in the dream told me that Eruch was related to my husband, and was also in some way connected to Baba, and that I must make it a point to go and meet him. The voice also assured me that I should not worry anymore about an issue that was bothering me a great deal at that time, because Baba had directed Eruch to take care of it.

The following day, I narrated the dream to Jehangir, and then to his sister, Shenaz, who lived in Pune and kept in touch with the people at Ahmednagar. I was amazed to learn that there was a person called Eruch, who had been a close follower and companion to Baba. I was also told that he was related to our family and lived in Ahmednagar with the rest of Baba's surviving Mandali.

That December, the much-anticipated trip to Ahmednagar took place. I was eager to meet Eruch, so we were directed to the Trust Office. No sooner did I enter the gates, I recalled that the big Banyan tree at the entrance was the same one I had seen in my dream, and the 'Eruch' I had visualised was as he looked from the old photos. A little awkwardly at first, I narrated my dream to him. For a moment, Eruch was nonplussed. Then he narrated an incident from Baba's days and said that, 'All Baba wants from us are our imperfections.' I interpreted this to mean that all He wants from me is to lay down at His feet my imperfections and ignorance, until I am washed clean of them.

A little later, we drove down to Pimpalgaon and Meherazad, Baba's home for many years. We walked around the gardens and visited Baba's room, sat at His dining table and felt the warmth of His home, and of His close followers. Our tour of Meherazad ended in the little hall where Eruch normally held his talks with visitors. Though there was no talk scheduled for that day, Bal Natu (one of Baba's Mandali and the author of a few Baba books), let us enter the Darshan Hall, which he specially opened for us. I stepped inside and something hit me so strongly that I sank down on the carpet in front of His armchair, adorned by His photograph and flowers. Suddenly, I seemed to have found that precious something I had been restlessly searching for so long ... Baba's Presence.

In early 1996, I was inspired to pick up a Baba book again, and its impact was just as dramatic! I had another dream in which I recalled being a ten-year-old girl in a family of Baba lovers. I saw Baba descend from a hill surrounded by a brilliant, flaming orange light. I was then introduced to various people as being members of my family and one lady in particular who was said to be my mother.

Less than a year later, Nan Umrigar's *Sounds of Silence* was published. Even before I could get a copy, I had the opportunity one afternoon to meet her at the Mahalakshmi Races. We only exchanged 'Hello's' but this meeting was to be unforgettable. I fondly recalled Nan's face that I had seen in the dream and known to be that of my mother! Despite this amazing encounter, my innate shyness prevented me from sharing my experience with her.

Almost two years passed. My father's fading health and resulting despondency finally urged me to seek help through Nan. I met and told her everything and she wrote to Karl for help for my father, which brought him solace and he faced the pain of his illness and the last months of his life with calmness and dignity.

However, hard times persisted. Confusion and inner turmoil led me to seek out meditation groups closer to home in my quest to make sense of the world around me and find inner peace. My health deteriorated and I withdrew into a shell – scared, depressed and feeling very, very alone. The medical reports left me devastated as I was diagnosed with a disease, which though in its preliminary stage, I hadn't expected to face at forty years of age.

Later that year when I felt well enough to travel, we made another trip to Ahmednagar. At Meherazad, one of Baba's women Mandali gave me a tiny box of Baba's special *Udhi* to take away and apply. Once again, overwhelmed by His love and compassion in reaching out to me through one of His people, I returned home with the thought that I have nothing to fear now.

Nearly a decade has passed since then. Life has moved on. Occasional health concerns persist, or the mind chatters incessantly. But amidst all this I am able to distinguish the thread of a voice; my own inner voice, my link with my higher Self, my Guardian Angels, my dear ones who have passed on, perhaps Karl, and yes, definitely Baba, helping me to reconnect with my Self. A connection that's so vital to my well-being and growth.

Arish Patel was one of those fortunate few souls born and brought up in a family in which spirituality played a very important part. It all started with his great grandfather, a spiritual seeker who died at a fairly young age; coming down to his grandfather, Hoshang Patel, who had met Baba in His physical form, and was a complete devotee; a man who lived his life with utmost sincerity and honesty; who believed that no matter what, Meher Baba is above everything and that truth always prevails. Till today, he loves and worships Meher Baba with complete sincerity and devotion. Arish's mother Villoo has now passed over to Baba, while his father Jimmy who I believe is a real *karma yogi*, silently works behind the scenes to carry on Baba's work.

Here is Arish's story ...

Arish Patel

As a child, going to Meherabad meant a great deal of enjoyment for me. It meant mixing with a lot of Baba friends, eating good food all through the day, and games of volleyball in the evenings. But we kids never really realised the importance that this place held for us, till Baba reached out to me in person through a book called *Sounds of Silence*.

I was twenty-two years old when I read this amazing book. Oh my God! It added so much more to my life. I, who had never read a book in my life, was glued to it for three days. Although I was led by my family to believe that Baba is God, it was never a confirmed fact for me. Therefore, this book helped tremendously to supplement my existing knowledge. From the day I finished the book, my faith in Baba has solidified so much that nothing in the world will ever change it. *Sounds of Silence* evoked a strong desire in me to serve Baba in some way. So, once I had thoroughly digested its contents, I decided that the best way to begin was that I should not keep this wonderful knowledge to myself. I was so impressed with the thoughts and feelings expressed in it, that I had to share it with all my friends and get them on track with the Lord. So I circulated the book and was stunned by the reaction. Everybody, just everybody I spoke to, wanted to come to this place called Meherabad. I was thrilled! This may seem unbelievable to you, but every time I still talk about *Sounds of Silence* to anyone, I get a shiver down my spine. I seem to feel the energy of Karl and the Divine Presence of Meher Baba all around me. Another amazing fact is that, to date, most of those whom I have spoken to have soon become Baba devotees and Baba's Grace has already started flowing into their lives.

I have also been the recipient of four beautiful letters of guidance from Karl that have helped me in my day-to-day life. He was not just a spirit presence; he was someone very special to me. I had never imagined that Baba would ever connect with His lovers using this medium, a method which I know a lot of old Baba lovers do not view with much favour, but I think it is time that we come to understand and accept that there is a lot of spiritual awareness in the world today, and that Baba has His own unfathomable ways of reaching out to us. Baba is a great communicator, no matter who or what the medium may be, and I feel this in my heart and I know it to be true. Very often, one finds oneself reading something that may be totally new; something one knows nothing about. But there is a deep sense of knowing; a deep feeling within which says, 'This is my truth.' And so it was with me. Baba always said that He would break His Silence one day, but He never did. However, I sincerely do believe that Baba makes us listen to the sounds of His sweetness through the pages of this book.

It was in the year 2000 when, during one of my annual visits to Meherabad, my dear friend Mehera Kliener came to me with the suggestion of helping organise a *Sahavas* for the first time in India at Meherabad. 'A Sahavas?' I thought to myself. I had heard about Sahavases happening all over the world but never knew what it exactly meant. So, Mehera explained that Sahavas meant being in the company of God, and that Baba in His physical form also used to have Sahavases very often with His followers at different destinations in India. Here was my opportunity to serve, and I jumped at it, knowing full well that Baba had heard my request.

In July 2000, we had our very first Young Adult Sahavas that was attended by ninety Meher Baba lovers, in the age group of nineteen to thirty-five years, and they came from all over the world. What an experience it was! I would give up lifetimes to relive those ten days in the Sahavas to be in the company of His lovers and, of course, our Beloved Baba.

I remember one particular incident that took place on the last day of the Sahavas at the Mandali Hall. *Diyas* were lit; Meher Baba's songs were being played by the *Sahavasis* and all of us were in a trance experiencing His Divine Love. While the songs were played, each Sahavasi was allowed to have a darshan at Baba's chair and received a gift that the Mandali had presented to each one. While all this was going on, one of the Sahavasis saw a kind of shadow sitting on Baba's chair and giving darshan to each Sahavasi – with a pat on the head, a pinch on the cheek, or a kiss on the forehead – while he bowed before the chair. He instantly realised that it was Baba giving darshan. When I bent down to take darshan, I also felt this immense pressure on my head and understood it was Baba's loving hand. My heart was full of His love.

Now I am into my fourth Sahavas. I try very hard during these days to do my level best to serve Beloved Baba, whether it is by playing His songs; getting ready for the dance night; photographing the entire event; acting in plays; and much more.

In one of His messages, Baba has said something to the effect of, *'The Sahavas never ends, only the programmes will, for each of My Sahavasis will take the Sahavas back home to his family and friends and that truly will be the real Sahavas.'*

So, in all humility, and in continuance of my service to Baba, I beg the young people who love Baba to try and take part in the Sahavas. Please leave everything behind – college, family, job, for a few days, and participate in this magnificent event, so that you can experience Meher Baba's Divine Love at its fullest.

My prayer to Him, as my grandfather instructed to pray every day, is: 'Help, guide and protect, for You only know what is best for me.'

I love Karl, my dearest brother in heaven, for showing me the way. I love my Beloved Meher Baba for the phenomenal Grace He showers on all of us.

CHAPTER 5

Two Friends and Baba

I am now going to narrate the stories of two friends who grew up in Dehradun together and whose families are also closely connected to Baba. These stories connect the past to the present as the Love of Baba has flowed like a beautiful river from the parent to the child who has since grown to love and serve Baba.

One bright September morning in 2011, my friend Rupam Nangia called up to tell me that there was a Baba meeting being held in the suburbs of Mumbai at the home of a lady called Meher Verma. 'Nan, you have to come,' she insisted. 'You will really enjoy listening to her stories. Most of those who are coming have also read your book *Sounds of Silence* and it will give them an opportunity to meet you, and listen to some of your new experiences. Please do come.'

Any opportunity to meet Baba followers is something I look forward to and, so, I found myself in Meher's lovely home in Lokhandwala Complex at Andheri in Mumbai. We were warmly welcomed by Meher and soon found ourselves well settled and listening to what Meher had to share with us.

Meher's family is from Dehradun and is closely connected with Meher Baba. How that connection happened formed the basis of her stories. She spoke with so much love and humour that I found myself totally absorbed. And I would like to share something of what I heard that day, with you.

34

Meher Verma (Her father's story)

This happened in the days when Baba used to go quite often to Dehradun with some of His Mandali and spend some time for His work there. Many people had heard of Him and this time the news also reached Meher's parents. Meher's mother, Prakashwati, being an ardent devotee of Lord Krishna, refused to believe in Baba and His Divinity unless she saw him in the form of the God she worshipped, who was Lord Krishna. Meher's father took some time to become a real Baba *bhakt* and, at the time of this story, had rather lukewarm feelings towards Baba.

One day when Baba needed a car to take some friends around, it was Meher's father, whom she called Bauji, who offered to drive them in his car; thinking that here was an opportunity to go along and spend some time in Baba's company.

But as luck would have it, Baba had too many companions and so He politely asked Bauji if he would follow them in the jeep. Much to his discomfort, Bauji soon realised that this

Bauji with Meher Baba.

journey was not going to be what he had thought it would be, for the jeep had no roof, the doors rattled and there was no front windshield to the jeep. The roads of Dehradun were not tarred at that time, so as the cars picked up speed the dust began to fly and his clothes got covered in dirt. Not just that, the muck went straight into Bauji's face, nose and eyes. The thoughts swirling in Bauji's head were not pleasant ones. He thought to himself, 'I really do not know if this is a God or what! That is my car, my driver, He is using my petrol, and here I am relegated to the back in this dirty jeep with all the dust flying in my face! Would He really do that if He were God?'

The journey in the jeep became even worse as the minutes sped by and Bauji even muttered a few swear words under his breath. But then, suddenly Baba's car stopped and one of the men got out. Then Baba indicated to Bauji that he could come and sit near Him, which he did with great relief. The cars started on their onward journey. Then Baba said to the gentleman sitting in the front seat, 'Kumar, there is a diary there. Could you please pick it up and read out aloud what is written inside?'

Kumar took up the diary and began to read: 'I do not know if this is a God or what ... This is my car, my petrol ... He is using my driver. Would He really do this if He were God?' Bauji squirmed in his seat and did not know where to look, especially when what followed were some of the swear words he had muttered, as well! He folded his hands and said, 'Maaf Karo, Baba!' (Forgive me, Baba!). He raised his eyes and saw a broad and most mischievous smile on Baba's face.

After this tale was over, the rest of the evening was spent listening to many other stories from Meher – stories that could fill up a whole book! I for one am after Meher to write them all down – right from the time she sat on Baba's lap as a three-month old baby caressed and loved by Baba, up to now when she spends so much time holding meetings at her residence in the service of Baba.

Both Meher and Amrit Irani's families lived in Dehradun. Amrit's association with Baba, much like Meher's, also happened through her father Shatrugan Kumar.

I know Amrit rather well. I have seen and met her in Meherabad and know of her association with Baba's family, through her marriage to Baba's nephew Dara Irani. However, I did not know much about her early life and connection to Baba, nor of the love that her own family had for Him. How that happened, starting with her father, is a fascinating story in itself and here I am reproducing it in his own words for you to read. He calls it, 'The Blessed Moments of Lifetimes'.

Amrit Irani (Her father's story)

In the 1930s, long before I had heard of Meher Baba, I, Shatrugan Kumar, was totally engrossed in politics and played an active part as a revolutionary in the fight to free India, my motherland, from British rule. I went to jail twice and altogether I was imprisoned for over ten years because of my political activities.

Arrested the second time in 1940, I was put in the Bareilly Jail of Uttar Pradesh. I did not have proper documentation and was simply incarcerated as a 'state prisoner' with no term set to my imprisonment. After five years, I learned that some leaders of the revolutionary movement were being released. As these men were considered far more dangerous by the government than me, who was not an important leader, I began to hope that I too would be released soon.

Instead of being freed, I was shifted to an underground cellar and placed in solitary confinement, from which prisoners generally had no hope of being released. I knew that for me, this was the end of the line. I thought of my young wife, Subhadra, and my widowed mother whom I loved dearly, having to till our farmlands, waiting patiently and hopefully for me to come home. But now, I thought I would never get to see them again.

I used to think that if I could only get out, I might even give up my revolutionary activities. I had grown tired of being in jail and had begun to crave freedom. But I knew it was no use thinking in such terms for there was no likelihood of my ever getting out, and my loved ones would never even know what had happened to me. One day, I suddenly sat up with a jerk and exclaimed, 'God ... only God, if He exists, can help me!' I thought that now the only way out of jail was to ask God to help me. I had been brought up in a spiritual environment at home but after joining the revolutionary party and spending a long time in politics, I had become an agnostic.

However, when the other prisoners were fast asleep that night, I prepared myself for the first time, to request something of God. I either didn't know, or by then had forgotten, how to address God, so I simply said, 'Mr. God, if there is a God, I request that you please get me released from this jail.' Simultaneous to this thought, came the thought that every pain and punishment is a result of a person's own karma according to his deeds. If prison was my own fate, then why should God interfere? But right on the heels of this thought, came another – that if I accepted some binding and promised to fulfil it if I got out of jail, then that would offset or repay my bad karma. I felt light at heart as I thought this was the right solution.

So I requested again, 'Mr. God, please get me released from this jail and in exchange I promise to abide by and obey any binding whatsoever, which You impose upon me outside this jail.' While I was asking this favour of God, I began to feel strongly that God was going to listen to and answer my prayer.

Then another thought entered my mind. 'How will I know if my bargain has been accepted by God? Even if I am released, what proof will I have that it was God's doing?' So I added, 'Please God, if You have accepted my promise and bargain, then get me released early in the morning as soon as the prison gates are opened. If I am released at any other time – the following day, tomorrow evening, or even a few hours after the gates open tomorrow morning, I will take it that my release was by chance, and not of Your doing.' Actually, it would be almost impossible for me to be released at dawn, for the superintendent, who would have to sign my release papers, never arrived till at least ten in the morning. Despite this, after negotiating so with God, I was sure that I would be released in the early hours of the morning, so I started to pack my belongings in two large trunks. I spent the whole night praying, requesting, promising, bargaining, and packing.

As dawn approached, I was becoming extremely anxious. Then I heard the key being turned in the lock, my cell gate opened, and a guard handed me a slip of paper on which was written, 'Mr. Kumar, get yourself ready with bag and baggage.' For a few minutes, I couldn't take it all in. I was trying to understand what was happening, when some prison officials came and took me to the superintendent's office.

I remember it was still dark and the lamp was burning in his office. The superintendent had me sign some papers for my release and travelling expenses. My trunks were given to two prisoners to carry, and I was allowed to pass out of the main gate and left there. I was free!

In the east the sky was just brightening. I think I must have been the only prisoner to be released at such an odd hour, just a few minutes before 5 am. To this day, I don't know what occurred to allow my release in this manner and at that time. I got a ride into town and caught a train for Dehradun. I was home the next day.

I have never forgotten my bargain and promise to God. In fact, I befriended many spiritual people and moved to my present home in the village Manjri Mafi, which is now called Meher Mafi. Five years later, towards the end of 1949, I saw a horse cart approaching my house. The people in it called me and asked if I could help them purchase some land in a few days' time. This was easy for me to arrange and within the stipulated time, they had bought the land.

They then asked if I could arrange for meals to be provided for a gentleman who was coming to live on the property they had acquired. I said I could do that, and to my surprise, they insisted on giving me five hundred rupees for this, in spite of my refusal to accept it. Some days later, the gentleman arrived. His name was Kaikobad Dastur. Either I, or someone in my family, would take food to him. One day, while I was sharing a cup of tea with him, he showed me a photograph of Meher Baba. He said that He is the Avatar, God in Human Form, and you are fortunate to serve Him. As for himself, he said, 'I am His slave.'

I don't know what happened but from that day, I began to see Meher Baba in my dreams every night, until I actually met Baba in person. Later, Baba himself asked me whether I had ever seen Him in my dreams. I replied, 'Yes.'

Baba said, 'As I am?'

I replied, 'No, Baba.'

I dreamt of You with a beard, looking very lean and thin. As if You had been fasting. Baba laughed at this and I thought I had said something foolish. But later on, I came across a Baba button, in which Baba had a beard and was very lean and thin, as I saw Him in my dreams. I bought that button and since then I have always kept it with me.

In 1954, about eight years after my release from prison, Baba called me to Satara in Maharashtra to spend one week with Him. But Baba kept me there for almost a year. He imposed some restrictions on me, such as: I would not correspond with anyone, and that I would not step out of the premises unless I was accompanying Him as His umbrella bearer.

Several months passed like this. My clothes were almost in rags, and I had grown a beard. One day it occurred to me that I had so many restrictions; it was as if I was back in the prison! I became upset. I had spent so many years in jail and now it seemed as though my life had not changed much. That very day, Baba took me along in His car while He went for *mast* work. On the way, Baba asked me, 'How long were you in prison?' Without thinking, I replied, 'More than ten years, on two occasions: the first time, I was released after completing my sentence but, on the second occasion, during the second World War, I was imprisoned for an indefinite period.' 'How did you get released then?' Baba asked.

All of a sudden, I remembered everything. I had completely forgotten my bargain with God, but now it all came back to me: my plea to God, my bargain, and my promise. I said, 'I requested God to release me.'

Baba gestured, 'Only requested? Didn't you say something more to God?'

I looked into Baba's eyes. He was smiling. I said, 'Yes, Baba, I also made a promise.'

'In what manner did you request God, and what was your promise to Him?' He asked.

I explained that I didn't know how to address God, so I had begun my request by saying 'Mr. God, if there is a God, I request that you please get me released from this jail. And in return for this, I promise to abide by any binding whatsoever imposed upon me outside jail.'

All along, Baba had been smiling but suddenly He became very serious. He took my right hand, placed it upon His, and made me repeat the promise three times.

'Don't break this promise,' He gestured. 'I am God, I am 'That God' to whom you made that promise. I have kept My side of the bargain. Now you keep yours.'

Something like an electric current passed through my body and I began to perspire until I was completely soaked. Baba then caressed me lovingly. Up till that time, I had served Baba and loved Him as my Master, but now I knew with conviction beyond question that I had found God, the Highest of the High. It was the most blessed moment of my lifetime.'

And now to get back to Amrit ...

While Kumar moved on to becoming Baba's umbrella bearer, his daughter Amrit grew up in the sheltered atmosphere of Dehradun. She went to school there and lived a happy life with her family.

While she was growing up she had more interaction with the women in Baba's Mandali than with Baba Himself. When she was eighteen years old, she got a letter one day from Baba saying something to this effect, 'I am not telling you, but asking you ... Will you marry My nephew Dara?'

Meher Baba with Kumar as His umbrella bearer.

Amrit was not shocked. She was in fact very happy to receive a letter from Baba asking her to marry Dara. At that time, Dara was still in the UK and did not return to India till close to the wedding date in December 1968. Amrit had grown up in a Hindi-speaking State, and her English was poor. Baba had told Amrit all about Dara before they met. He had also told her that Dara had weak eyesight and would most likely go blind, so she had been prepared by Baba about the life that lay ahead of her.

Such was her obedience and love for Baba that without any hesitation she said, 'Yes,' to the proposal of marriage. How she met Baba, how Baba arranged the whole wedding function, how He organised everything right down to the colour of the *sari* she was to wear, and performed the whole ceremony Himself – that is a story in itself. Although Dara has now lost his eyesight completely, she leads him everywhere and they are quite happy with each other. They live in a beautiful house just below Meherabad Hill with their two lovely children. Maybe one day, when you are in Meherabad, you can go and share a cup of tea with them and Amrit could tell you the rest of her story. You can see her presiding at 6 am over the tomb's cleaning at the Samadhi. Her service to Baba is selfless and her love for Him always shines through.

Many Happy Returns…
Past and Present

Man or mouse, everyone born into this world must eventually pass away. The end of life comes to one and all. What is important is how, where, and when it happens. Probably the most painful is the loss of a parent and more so of a child, especially if it happens early in life, or if it is a sudden passing.

Sounds of Silence was written after my son Karl was killed in a riding accident on the racecourse in 1979. This book told how Meher Baba came into my life, healed my aching heart, and introduced me to a new concept – called *auto writing,* a process which makes it possible to contact someone even though that person is not in physical form anymore. It proved to be the beginning of a new life for me, as well as for so many others who followed.

Then came *Listening to the Silence* in which I shared all my sad thoughts, as well as my doubts and fears, with all of you. It also acquainted you with the personal experiences of others who, after reading of my attempts, started to walk the same path and began to make their own way forward. But what form will it take? Baba works with each individual so differently. To most, Baba has sent loving messages from those passed over. Some persons, like me, reconnected by means of auto writing, some by dreams, some by promises of a meeting when their own life in the world is over; and so on. But nobody's story is ever the same. It does not stop there; it goes beyond …

Here are two more miraculous stories, one from the past when Meher Baba was in His physical body, and one from 2010. They both drive home the point that no one person is the same as the other to Baba; that each one of us has to follow Him inwardly; that Baba deals with a situation according to the need of the hour; and that nothing is impossible for Him.

43

Kusum Singh (Her mother's story)

The mansion of Maharani Mohini of Sahanpur was adjacent to Meher Baba's bungalow at 101 Rajpur Road in Dehradun. Mohini lived with her husband, Charat Singh, the Raja of Sahanpur. One of her daughters, Pushpa Lata, was married to the Maharaja of Patiala, but the young woman had died during childbirth. Overcome with grief, the Maharani became mentally unstable and would probably have become deranged had she not met Baba around that time.

One evening, the Maharani, accompanied by her husband, visited Meher Baba at His bungalow. Eruch, who was sitting outside on the veranda with Baba, enquired the purpose of their visit. Mohini said, 'Baba, I have come to You in great misery. I have one simple request to ask of You.' Baba gently asked, 'What is it? What do you want from Me?'

'I cannot live without my daughter, Baba ... I want my daughter back. I implore you to bring my daughter back to life!' Saying this, Mohini started weeping as she narrated her story. Baba comforted her with the words, 'Why do you cry? You will have your daughter back.'

Mohini was startled to hear these words and asked, 'The same daughter, Baba? In the same physical form?'

'Yes, the same daughter,' He promised.

'But Baba, her body has been cremated!' wailed Mohini

Baba smiled, and His smile dissolved Mohini's anguish. He said, 'I am *Paramatma*, and nothing is impossible for Me.' He further assured her, 'I have created the universe! Can I not make your daughter come alive?'

These words lifted the terrible burden from her heart, and in her despair she now saw a ray of hope. Wonderstruck at Baba's words, she asked, 'Would You truly give me back my daughter?'

Baba again gave her a reassuring smile, 'Yes, I am telling you exactly that. Now stop worrying and have patience. Your daughter will come back to you. All you have to do is to remember Me and love Me. Remember Me constantly and love Me as much as you can, more and more each day. Will you do that?'

The Maharani agreed and feeling light at heart for the first time, she and her husband left for their home. Eruch, who had been interpreting Baba's words, had been stunned and was thinking: 'My God! What is Baba promising? It is not like Him to declare such things.' He said to Baba, 'You have assured the Maharani that her daughter will come back, but what will happen when she does not come back?'

Baba replied, 'I have the remedy for every disease, and My treatment is infallible. At present, she needs this medicine until her illness subsides. She was happy and you will see that her condition won't worsen; on the contrary, it will improve.'

Some days later, Mohini came to Baba and said that she wished to sweep and clean His room herself. When Baba agreed to this, she began to clean it. She then asked for some personal article of Baba's, and was given His *sadra*.

As long as Baba was in Dehradun, Mohini was happy and inwardly had started depending more and more on Him. After Baba left, she would write to Him whenever she thought of her daughter. Baba would reply that she must be patient; her daughter would definitely return to her; and in the meantime she should go on thinking of Him. Baba indicated that she would see her daughter in a dream and that this would be the sign of her imminent return.

Sometime in 1954, the Maharani came to Ahmednagar along with her husband for Baba's darshan, determined to ask Him to finally bring her daughter back from the dead. But in Baba's presence, she completely forgot to ask about it.

Some years later, when the couple came to Guruprasad, which was the Maharani of Baroda's palace in Pune and was used by Baba for His darshan, He asked Mohini, 'How are you?'

'Baba, I am very happy,' she answered.

Baba looked radiant that day and suddenly told her, 'I am in the mood at this moment to give you whatever you ask. Tell me at once: do you want your daughter back, or do you want Me?'

The Maharani gently placed her hand on Baba's knee and answered, 'I want You, Baba.' To that, Baba replied, 'Now you have your daughter back. The whole world is in Me, including your daughter.'

Because of her daughter's death, Mohini came into close contact with Baba and became His forever. Her husband, Charat Singh, also held fast to Baba's feet, and their other daughter, Kusum, also came into the fold of Baba's Love. Kusum's husband, Sardar Mohkam Singh, at first had no faith in Baba but, once when he was brought for darshan, he was so strongly drawn to Baba that he made it a rule to periodically arrange *bhajan-kirtan* programmes at their residence in New Delhi.

Maharani Mohini's elder sister, Rama Devi of Mukimpur, in Bulandshahar District, and her family, also came into contact with Baba. Around fifty of her other relatives had the good fortune to be at Baba's feet, because of the death of Pushpa Lata.

Thus was the daughter of Mohini brought to life by Meher Baba's Love.

One evening a fancy, big Mercedes drove into the parking lot of my home and a gentleman stepped out of the car. He had come at the appointed time for a meeting with me and had been referred by my niece Abe Dubash Meresh from Delhi. He was middle-aged, well-spoken, intelligent, and had the confidence of someone used to getting his own way. He indicated that being an independent advocate at the Supreme Court in Delhi, he was well-versed with the laws of the land. It was apparent that he possessed the ability to hold his own amongst a gathering. As far as spiritual knowledge was concerned, he considered himself theoretically sound, and had good contacts among various saints, spiritual personalities, and leading astrologers. But the hollowness of all that theoretical knowledge became painfully clear to him when he lost his child – and that is why he was here.

His eldest son, Shaunak, had passed away during a bout of fever and he was now in search of some way to get in touch with him. Abe had given him my book *Sounds of Silence* and from the conversation that ensued, he seemed to already have a good idea about Meher Baba. So, at that moment, all I could do was direct him towards Baba's Samadhi at Meherabad, Ahmednagar, with the assurance that a message would soon follow.

Karl's message, when it came, said: *'Baba is very aware of all those who are hurting and want to have some news about their loved ones after they leave this world. He would like very much to bring the two worlds together, so that human beings will not feel so devastated when their loved ones pass away. Baba sees so much pain when that happens, that now He has diverted His attention to this more than ever before. He wants people to know that there is no such thing as gone forever — only Love is forever — and that is exactly what Baba is here to prove.'*

What will be narrated now may seem to be straight out of some mythology text, but it will prove that Makarand and his wife Yogini were chosen to take part in a Divine drama, with Meher Baba as its controller and director. Baba not only demonstrated the closeness of the two worlds, but went out of His way to make them understand that there indeed exists an interaction between them and how it actually takes place.

Makarand Adkar

I was born and brought up in Pune. I was a good student and had got a First Class in the M.A. examination. I also stood First in the Law exam after which I completed my M.Com with distinction. I belong to the third generation of a family of advocates and, after finishing my studies, opted to practice Law. In January 1988, I moved to Delhi without any financial or family support. In the beginning, I went through a tough time, to the extent of going without food or proper shelter for days together, but as I was meant to settle in Delhi, destiny supported me and within a year of apprenticeship in the Supreme Court, I became an independent Advocate.

I married Yogini, a year later on 30th October, 1989, and settled down at Noida near Delhi. We had two sons named Shaunak and Shantanu. Shaunak was a beautiful and exceptionally straightforward boy. I always worried how such a simple boy would cope with the ruthlessness of the society in which we live nowadays.

A curious aspect of my life's journey is that during the past ten years, I had suddenly developed an interest in the teachings of various religions and, for no apparent reason, I started studying subjects like death and what happens thereafter.

In 2009, we moved to a much larger home. By this time, I had already opened offices in Pune as well as in Dubai. Although life became hectic with me having to travel extensively, things were going well and we were a happy and contented family. That is until that day in November of the same year when I had to go for some work to Pune. I returned to Delhi the next day to find that Shaunak was not feeling well. He was extremely irritable and appeared to be drained of physical energy. It took a lot of effort to persuade him to accompany me to a doctor whose clinic was just adjacent to our home. Shaunak was diagnosed to be suffering from Dengue and his platelet count had dropped well below normal. However, the doctor felt that his condition was not alarming and that we could wait till the next morning to repeat the test for platelet count.

On 12th November, it was found there was bleeding when Shaunak went to the bathroom. The doctor said that Shaunak would now need to be given intravenous platelet transfusions. Since my blood group matched, I was naturally the donor. During all this time, Shaunak remained very depressed and kept asking us to take him home. That night at 10 pm, following the administration of an injection by the resident doctor, Shaunak collapsed. Later around midnight, we shifted Shaunak to Fortis Hospital where the doctors informed us that Shaunak's condition was critical.

We were stunned. We just kept witnessing what was happening and simply followed the instructions that were given by the doctors. Those nights completely drained our mental, physical and emotional states. We didn't know where else to seek help. Who could we turn to? On the one hand, our child was battling for his life and, on the other, Yogini and I were running around trying to contact the various saints and astrologers we knew and whom we hoped may help save our child. I went to meet a prominent astrologer who closed his eyes for a few minutes, and then asked me to perform some complex rituals to propitiate the gods. By dawn, Yogini had somehow reached the Saint of Shantikunj and sought his blessings of a long life for our child. But the blessings did not come in the way we expected, for he told her that all happens according to the Divine Will. Being a mother, Yogini then realised what was going to happen.

Around 11 am, I entered the ICU and just then, at that very moment, the machine started beeping, indicating that our child's heart had stopped beating. I was stunned and stood frozen in my tracks. The doctor started reviving the heart and I was dragged out of the room. I sat in the corridor trying to understand what had happened. I looked around and saw Yogini at the end of the corridor anxiously making gestures indicating that she also wanted to come into the ICU, but the security guard would not allow anyone to go in.

Looking back, I shudder to think of what all Yogini and I went through that night. Yet, the fact remains that the physical body of our child was soon turned into ashes and we would never see his beautiful, smiling face ever again. We never imagined that we could carry on living and leading our normal lives without Shaunak. However, Divinity has its own ways of ending a young man's journey and prolonging that of older ones. All the theoretical knowledge that I had gained from reading various religious scriptures and books on death and the afterlife did not come to my rescue, nor offer solace in my hour of need.

Shaunak, our precious child, left his physical form on 13th November 2009, and I do not know how we lived through our days thereafter. However, time doesn't stand still and the days kept on passing. Nine days later, we had a condolence meeting at our residence and here Yogini totally let go of all restraint and cried like a child. I really do not know who or what prompted me, for it was certainly not the place nor the time to ask her such a question, but I suddenly went up to her, and putting my arms around her, asked her if she wanted to communicate with our child. She looked up at me through her tears and nodded a 'Yes'!

That same evening of November 22, my advocate friend Meenakshi Arora happened to visit us. She mentioned the name of one Mrs. Abe Dubash who had a link with the *spirit world*. In other words, Abe Dubash could connect and communicate with higher level souls in the spirit world and we could get guidance from them through her. The next day, I contacted the lady who asked me to read *Sounds of Silence* by Nan Umrigar. Yogini and I rushed to a bookstore to get copies of this book and read the story of a young boy called Karl Umrigar, who communicates with his mother. As you will see later, this book not only helped to strengthen our belief that communication is possible, but it also proved to be a milestone in our future progress, and changed the entire course of our lives.

We kept in touch with Mrs. Dubash and I must say that her guidance proved to be priceless. With the help of her communication, she kept us updated with the progress of our son in the spirit world. It began with letting us know that the soul of our child was at rest and absolutely safe. And so it went on, till one day in her communication, Shaunak spoke of an anniversary card which he had bought for our wedding anniversary in October and had wanted to give us, but for some reason it could not be given to us.

Eagerly, we looked around for the card but could not find it. We were not only saddened; we also began to doubt the whole process. Was communication between two worlds really possible? However, the card remained at the back of our minds. By the end of January 2010, we decided to move from our new big house back to the old small house. Yogini got busy sorting and packing things. One morning I suddenly heard Yogini calling me, and her voice sounded just the way it would when she would see Shaunak. She had found that anniversary card in Shaunak's papers! Can you imagine our joy at that moment! Our faith in the authenticity of our message from Shaunak was reinforced.

Sometime in mid-December 2009, I had suddenly mentioned to Yogini that we should have another child. It was strange that I should even think of this, given that both of us were around fifty years old, and had lost our dear son just a month earlier. What was even stranger was Yogini's response – she had replied in the affirmative! Then Yogini consulted her friend Dr. Leena Jadhav who, in turn, directed us to Dr. Mangla Telang for further guidance. During the consultation he explained to us the pros and cons, and then advised us to reconsider our decision.

Here, I should mention that from 13th November 2009, I had once again started contacting saints, spiritual personalities and top astrologers to gain guidance and insights as to why events had occurred the way they did. Thus, the day on which we met Dr. Mangla Telang, we were actually supposed to meet a saintly person known as Babaji at the residence of Devendra Mishra in Ghaziabad. It was here that we also met Swami Rambhadracharyaji, Shankaracharya of Tulsi Peeth, Chitrakoot, U.P.

After we had narrated our situation to Swamiji, he asked me to come close to him and silently murmured something in my ear. He asked me whether I would like to have my child back! I immediately answered in the affirmative. Then Swamiji asked both of us to see him the next morning where he performed an elaborate *puja* of Lord Bal Krishna. After it was over, he asked me to come close to him and once again murmuring into my ear he said that God would surely perform a miracle. I mentioned that I was very concerned for Yogini, as both of us were fifty years old, but Swamiji assured us that a way would present itself after consultation with the doctors, and that all would be well. Here, I should add that although Swami Rambhadracharyaji is a well-known spiritual authority, he is blind. One of his close disciples informed me that while Swamiji was accustomed to hearing strange stories, he was somehow very upset and moved after hearing about our experience.

Almost immediately after Shaunak left us, the Divine in Its wisdom had diverted our attention to another serious incident. On 14th November 2009, some friends had gathered at our residence to keep us company, when my sister who had come from Mumbai noticed that our younger child, Shantanu, who was fourteen years old, was looking weak. They took Shantanu to Max Hospital where the doctors advised we admit him. We were shocked when the doctors told us that Shantanu had Dengue! Shantanu was kept in hospital for a week and after further tests we were told he had the Swine Flu. It took a fortnight for him to recover.

In *Sounds of Silence*, we are told that Meher Baba had declared that He came 'Not to Teach, but to Awaken.' He only insisted that every human being should strive to be one with God through love. We came to understand that He was even now working hard to bring the physical and non-physical worlds together. This is the path that Yogini and I now began to follow in real earnest.

In mid-December 2009, I had contacted Mrs. Umrigar and she had told me to email her a short note on Shaunak's departure from this world. I sent this to her and soon her son, Karl, in the spirit world, located our child and the most gracious Avatar Meher Baba started visiting our child to take care of him.

We received our first message from Karl on 2nd January 2010, an extract from which is posted here:

'Your son has progressed very fast. Of course he is still resting but his status has changed from being inert to being alert. He is slowly getting aware of his surroundings and has come to realise Baba's touch very well. So when Baba comes and sits near him and tenderly hugs him, he immediately reacts. He listens to Baba like a son to a father.'

On 21st January 2010, Karl further informed us:

'Dear Yogini and Makarand, you have a very good child who is going to be of great help to anyone who comes in contact with him. He will be everyone's lucky charm until all his lifetimes are over and many will call him for help in their times of trouble. We call him 'Angel Wings' because he is like an angel who flies everywhere and does so much for everyone.'

Of course we could hardly wait until the rest period was over and, sure enough, we soon received a message through Karl in which our child addressed us both, saying:

'Dearest Mummy and Daddy, I know how much you both are hurting and so was I till dearest beloved Baba explained to me that all this is just a temporary parting and nothing permanent. Believe me mummy, when I say that there is a life after death and there is no such thing as gone forever. I see Baba every day helping so many and He wants that we too can help Him to help those that need help.'

Once during a discussion with the astrologer, I was told that my child wished to come back to his parents. And further, the astrologer went on to say that if our child was interested in our spiritual progress, then we would have a daughter and we should name her Anusuya. Should it be a boy then the name of any saint would do. The most relevant point here is that in the case of a daughter, a specific name was suggested.

It was around this time that I was also given a book titled *The Laws of the Spirit World*. It talks about Mrs. Bhavnagri's contact with her deceased sons. Her work is now being carried on by Shiamak Davar, the famous dance choreographer, who continues to help people the way she used to. I tried to contact Shiamak and he asked me to meet him during his vacation in Mahabaleshwar. When we met, he explained that my child in heaven had organised our meeting. I was also told that souls make a plan in the astral world before being born and that Shaunak's passing away was a part of this plan. I requested Shiamak to talk with Yogini and, during the telephone conversation, she asked him pointedly as to whether she would get her child back. Shiamak explained to Yogini that now because our child was being placed on a higher level in the astral world, he would not like to come back. However, he informed me that the mechanism of the spirit world was such that if Yogini decided to bear a child, then no other soul would come to Yogini without the consent of Shaunak. He also mentioned that if and when a mother decides to bear a child again, then due to the karmic bond, the possibility of the same soul coming back cannot be ruled out.

In addition to all this, we were surprised to receive a message from Mrs. Abe Dubash that our child wanted to see us and meet us in Kolkata on a particular day, in a specific church. So I went to Kolkata and stayed there for some time and, interestingly, all of us experienced a mental state in a trance where we felt that we met our child. In this meeting we also requested our child to come back to us. For reasons known only to the Divine, some special energy was prompting Yogini and me to call our child back. It may sound strange to some that we were requesting people here and there for getting our child back, as if he had gone on some vacation! But both of us were confident that somehow, somewhere, our child would come back to us.

Towards the end of February 2010, Yogini had decided to conceive under the guidance of Dr. Mangla Telang and Dr. Leena Jadhav and these efforts were not known to anyone except us.

On 14th March 2010, we received another message from Shaunak through Karl: 'I have lived many times before. Now Baba will help me to finish my tenure of existence. I know that I still have one more long life ahead of me, where it is not going to be easy but I am not going to shy away from anything. I have faith in God, in the universe and in you my darling parents.'

On 23rd March 2010, our child sent another message through Karl which read: 'Dearest mummy and daddy, we have so much to look forward to and so much to do. I am extremely anxious to get on with it. I am well. I am happy and am convinced that as soon as you get better and a little stronger, we can all be a happy family once again.'

Now, at our request, Nan Umrigar connected Yogini to our child in heaven. With his permission, and under the umbrella of Avatar Meher Baba, she made the necessary connection for us and Yogini started automatic writing and got in direct touch with our child. The first few days were only practice sessions during which, just scrawling lines and mixed up letters appeared. However, within a month's time, words began to appear on the paper and the child started expressing his thoughts.

Some messages sent by Shaunak to his mother through auto writing:

24.03.2010

'I am with Baba and Karl. We have to perform so many tasks daily. Baba guides us how to help others, who call for help. It is a team-work and sometimes individual. It gives us great pleasure to help those who are in need. We will all serve Baba the way He wants and tell others to serve Him. This will help us to go step by step close to Him.'

26.03.2010

'I know the questions you want to ask me momma ... Just remember that this was to happen so it did. It is for our betterment and now that I am coming back, it will be just as it was before ... Keep calm; don't get disturbed with things around you. Speak less think more. Mummy lots and lots of love ... Momma distribute Baba's book to as many people.'

03.04.2010

When Yogini asked Shaunak how the system of birth and death is functioning for the people in general, she got this message: '... It depends where they stand. They do have to take rebirth to shed off all their karmas ... the system works that way. Few are chosen to stay back. Everything is set perfect here. You cannot cheat here. It is coming and going. Each time settling of your account and opening a new one with some previous balances to be set off ...'

05-04-2010

'I am very happy momma. I enjoyed so much yesterday ... playing with Tanu (Shantanu) made me really very happy too.'

15.04.2010

'There is no uncertainty mom, I am coming ... As parents I need your help. You will have to guide me so well that I lead the right path and achieve my goal. I am sure that you will take all the care and with Baba's blessings we will all lead a beautiful and meaningful life ...'

Yogini was now pregnant and we were delighted. However, the mind loves playing tricks on us and, being an Advocate, I constantly felt the need for confirmation about this new soul who would soon be with us. Once again, I requested Nan for a message from Karl. This time, the message was surprisingly different and very cautiously worded.

17.04.2010

Karl wrote: *'Your son has a path to follow. He is choosing it with great care and has to go forward with a brave heart.'*

So then, imagine our dismay when on 18th April 2010, during a routine sonography, Dr. Telang discovered an absence of foetal heartbeats. We were devastated and as soon as we got home, Yogini sat down to communicate with our son.

The message she got back was: 'Somebody is intervening in this decision. I do not know mom, I will try to find out. Somebody is trying to read your mind and trying to obstruct.

Keep calm momma. I will be back. I will work hard and protect you all from the evil. Don't lose hope, Baba is with us. Keep faith in Him.'

On my part, I immediately spoke over the phone with Swami Rambhadracharyaji and I explained the situation to him. I also mentioned that Dr. Telang had suggested that the procedure to terminate the pregnancy could be taken immediately. However, he had added that, 'Let us wait and see what God wills.' When Swamiji heard what I had to say, he scolded me and said that I should listen to him and not to the doctor. Swamiji asserted that all was well with our baby and we should forget what the doctor said.

An assurance from Swamiji was really the test of our faith in Divinity vis-a-vis the thinking capability of a rational mind. However, we let the situation remain as it was till the next sonography that was scheduled on 22nd April.

On 19th April, we got a message from Shaunak saying, 'I am OK. I am confused momma. Just wait. Do your prayers. Follow Meher Baba's path. I know it is difficult to bear this uncertainty but you have to wait for the right time. And right time is soon to come.'

On 21st April, while communicating with Shaunak, there was an intervention from Karl saying, *'Hello, it's me Karl. Your son is doing very well here. He is a bit confused. But Baba is there to guide him. You need not worry. He is in two minds. He knows he has to come back, only the time is not certain. He loves you a lot. Pray hard to Baba. He will fulfill your wish. He has some plans for your son. Let them work it out, then your son will be back to you as he will be there for a mission. Baba's mission which you both will have to support. I will remain in touch with you some way or the other.'* Then Shaunak wrote, 'I will discuss with Baba today and surely let you know. I am coming, just a little confused about the timing ...'

On 22nd April, before going for her sonography, Yogini communicated with Shaunak and he wrote: 'Hi momma, how are you? Yes there is going to be a miracle from Baba. His blessings are with you. Yes, I have been granted permission from Baba to come back ... Take care of your diet and health. You need to be fit and healthy.'

We held our breath as the sonography was performed and, truly, there was a miracle. The foetus was normal, the heartbeats were clearly audible and, when we received the report, there was a beautiful impression of Baba's face so clearly visible on the document.

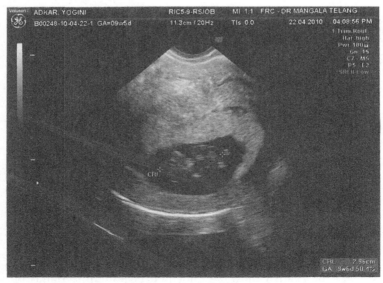

The image from the sonography showing Baba's face.

Under instructions from Nan Umrigar, I now planned my first visit to Meherabad. I was even able to meet Bhau Kalchuri, the head of the Trust. On hearing my story, he welcomed me with a warm Baba hug, allowed me to garland Baba's picture, and welcomed me into the fold.

23.4.2010

A message from Shaunak: 'You know momma, I was really not understating what to do. Life here is beautiful ... but I miss you so much; moreover I could not see you in pain. I had to decide to come back. And with Baba's blessings everything will be perfect. Follow your routine strictly. Things will now move very smoothly. All you have to do so is continuously be under Baba's guidance and care ...'

24.4.2010

Message from Karl sent through his mother: *'Dear Mr. Makarand, All is going to be well. Baba is looking into everything so that things go according to the needs of both parties. Baba is very aware of the implications of what is desired by you, but also has to see what is best for the child, so that his future growth and progress does not get affected in any way. He has to look to him not only at a human level but also as a soul. Your son has reached a high level here and Baba has to find a way of keeping him that way. Therefore He is looking at all the different ways of pleasing everyone and making it all into a loving and pleasing experience for all.'*

A strange event that occurred deserves a mention here. Before Sai Baba dropped his body, he handed over nine coins to Laxmi Bai who had served him food for forty years. These coins were given to Shailla Amma, the granddaughter of Laxmi Bai. While in Delhi, Shailla got a strong urge to visit us via a common friend. She gave those nine coins to Yogini, who held them close to her chest while Shailla Amma claimed she really could not understand what force brought her to us. She felt that Sai Baba had guided her to us, to bless us.

By the end of May 2010, Yogini was in the fourteenth week of her pregnancy. Her communication with the child kept Yogini mentally balanced and emotionally strong.

On 5th June, Karl one day alerted us with a message sent through his mother: *'The communication is going to get weaker day by day and then come to a stop. Soul is transferring slowly and so, cannot keep the link going. It will not be possible. So please take it as it comes and know that somewhere you need to say bye to him so that he can rest and grow. So be happy to feel the movements and then do the needful for him.*

Baba's love will keep you going as much as possible.'

On 25th July, Shaunak communicated with his mother for the last time by saying, 'Life is going to be very beautiful momma, and we will care for each other. Together we will achieve our goal. Proceed on our mission – 'Baba mission'. Baba will guide us from time to time. Remember Baba's every step, taking His guidance and blessings, is what we have to do.'

Towards the end of July, Yogini found that communication with Shaunak became weak and she did not get the signals as she would before. I asked Nan to request Karl if he could find out what was happening with our child.

Thus Karl on 6th August 2010 communicated: *'Dear Yogini and Makarand, Baba is happy with all that has taken place. At present the child is in its growing process, so we do not probe into what is going on between the soul and Baba, but so far all is going well and things seem to be in control. We do miss the presence of Shaunak here, but life has to go on and His wish and will has to be paramount.'*

Dr. Madhu Roy, Yogini's gynaecologist, decided it was best that a caesarian be performed on 5th November. As her time drew near, I felt urged to go to Meherabad. I planned to reach at noon and hoped to have a peaceful darshan of Baba, but it turned out to be much more than that. I entered the Samadhi room, knelt down, and had barely touched my forehead to the tombstone when suddenly I got a whiff of a strange fragrance – something I had never felt before. I was overcome and sat down abruptly near the tomb, knowing beyond a doubt that some experience of a Divine nature had taken place. It was much later that I came to know that many people experience a sweet fragrance when Ascended Beings are hovering nearby.

It was nearing October and we were getting physically, mentally and emotionally prepared to welcome our child. We made conscious efforts to keep the atmosphere at home as peaceful as possible by chanting mantras or listening to cassettes/ CDs of the mantras.

On 15th October, while at the airport in Pune, I received an urgent call from Yogini saying that she was feeling uneasy and was going to Apollo Hospital. How I wished I was with her at this moment.

On the 16th, the doctor decided that a caesarian section would be necessary. This is an important date in the life of Avatar Meher Baba, when in 1949, He, along with a few of His companions, embarked upon what He termed as the 'New Life'. This is also the date of Navami in Navaratri when the goddess is supposed to be most powerful. Yogini was taken into the operation theatre at about 9 am and at exactly 10:38 am our child, as promised and blessed by Avatar Meher Baba, came back to us in the form of a beautiful girl child who was to be named 'Anusuya'.

I called Nan to give her the good news and she said that she knew it was to be a girl. On 22nd October, Karl has sent us a message through his mother stating:

'Dear Yogini and Makarand, Baba has once more blessed you with a loving child and we are going to watch her grow with great care. This soul has come to you because of love – to love you, look after you and keep you always connected with Baba's love. She has come to bring joy and peace in your life again.

Baba and I and all of us here will miss this loving soul who enriched our lives so much here, but wanted to be with you to help you carry on your life in the world and to pass on good thoughts, good words and do good deeds to all those that come to you. Baba sends you greetings and wishes you many happy days with your loved ones.'

———————

It was in this way that the lives of Yogini and Makarand took a most unexpected turn and they became parents again at the age of fifty plus. It is not easy to describe their emotional and mental state, for no matter the time and place, to lose a young child tears at every parent's heart. But one thing is for sure. The timely coming of Meher Baba into their lives has changed it all for them, as it has done for so many, although in different ways.

Makarand is a changed person now. He has virtually stopped going to the courts and somehow lost the desire to shine in his profession. He does not take up any and every case that comes to him, but prefers to be like a beacon on the horizon, a light in the darkness, to lead any wayfarer to go the right way – towards Meher Baba's way. He prefers to stay more at home and spend his days with Yogini in happy contemplation of Anusuya's growth, and Shantanu's progress. His aim is to eventually become 'desireless' and find his happiness more in the simple things of life – like gazing upon his daughter and marvelling at the amazing similarity of appearance between her and Shaunak – extremely fair, blue eyes – their baby photographs are so identical. You may think it is just the fond hope or imagination of doting parents, but even casual friends and visitors have noticed this.

Let me add here that there was a big question mark as to whether the Adkars should share their story with others. Yogini was against it, and I was not sure how it would affect other readers who had lost their young children. It definitely needed some kind of an explanation that this was a rare case and that Baba does not make it a regular practise to bring babies/souls back to their parents. So, as always, we went back to Karl to let Baba make the decision for us, and this is what Karl said:

'Dear Makarand, You can reveal to people all that has happened in your life up to this day. To show how the coming of Baba has affected your whole life and family. In short, you are there to make Baba more accessible to others. So it is OK. You have Baba's permission to say whatever you feel is right. Really, we are not unduly worried for Baba would not have chosen you for this role if He did not have confidence in you.

Please know that Baba loves you, not only for yourself but also as a family – including the little new addition who is going to be Baba's ambassador, sent from here to prove a point, that actually the two worlds are not really separate, and that even if your loved ones do leave this physical world, they are not really gone forever.'

CHAPTER 7

Terror in Mumbai

I was peacefully reading a book one evening when a telephone call suddenly shattered the silence. 'Put on the TV ... Quick! Mumbai is burning!'

I panicked. 'My God! Mumbai burning?' I dashed across to the TV and switched on the news channel that was telecasting a view of the Taj Mahal Hotel covered with smoke and with huge, orange tongues of flame flaring out from its roof.

I lay awake the whole night seeing these horrific scenes on television. It seemed like a nightmare and I was numb with disbelief. The scenes kept shifting from the Oberoi Hotel, to the Leopold Restaurant at Colaba, and the Chhatrapati Shivaji Terminus (VT) – people were running helter-skelter, firemen were risking their lives while fighting the raging fires, sirens of ambulances were screaming as they ferried the wounded, women and children crying, and the media hovering around with their mikes for media bytes and as much live coverage and sensational news as they could possibly get amid all the confusion. One felt the anxiety, suspense, and grief of family members who waited outside for news of their loved ones who were either being held hostage in the hotels, or those who were difficult to trace at the sites of the attacks.

I don't need to go over all that again ... the whole world knows about the ghastly terror attacks that took place on that night of 26th November 2008. Till today, it is unknown how many people died, were wounded or injured, and of the heroic ones who lost their own lives while trying to save the lives of others.

Two stories illustrate how Baba reached out to those who were destined to be at that very place on that day, and at that time. At such times, it is so hard to believe or find consolation when we are told that even this is a part of the Divine plan and that – whether we like it or not, or believe it or not – the plan is perfect. Many are the lessons that are learnt and several achieve their spiritual growth through tragedies.

Shahnaz Jehani

As a kid, I used to attend all Baba's functions held either at Sunderbai Hall or Cama Hall, and visit the Meher Baba Centre at Navyug Niwas Society in Mumbai. For me it was a family outing. I never gave it much thought after returning home from the Centre. For me, it was like visiting any other temple with my family.

23rd November 2007 was a day which changed my entire life. It was a day that brought me closer to my God Meher Baba. Until then, I was a devout follower of Iranshah and would yearn to relate to Him, and for Him to show Himself to me in human form.

My husband Farzad and I were holidaying at my cousin Simin's house in New Jersey, USA. Simin is a Baba follower and she kept suggesting that since I had come all the way to New Jersey, I must make a trip to the Baba Centre at Myrtle Beach, South Carolina. However, I evaded the topic since I was a follower of Iranshah. Besides, our travel plans were fixed and we were to be in California in a week's time. But Baba had His own plans for me.

We got news that my brother-in-law had taken seriously ill and was taken to the hospital in Mumbai, and were asked to rush back home. We immediately cancelled our tickets to California and tried to get seats to fly back to Mumbai, but were told that all flights were going full. We didn't give up our efforts to obtain tickets and, after two days, we got a call that all was well with my brother-in-law and that he was getting discharged from the hospital.

We were now left stranded. What should we do? Simin had already planned to drive to the Meher Spiritual Centre at Myrtle Beach. She suggested that we could join her, but I was apprehensive. My knowledge of spiritual matters at that time did not allow me to understand that all Masters are one, and it matters not who we bow down to and follow. Unknown to me, Meher Baba was drawing me closer to Him and convincing me that my Iranshah and He are one. I can only say that this trip was entirely His doing and it transformed my life. Returning to Mumbai, I visited Meherabad and bowed down. I had found my Master, my Friend, my Companion and, most importantly, I had found my God and it was He who saw me through the trials of 26/11.

So much about myself, and how I came to Baba.

I am now here to tell you about what happened to me and my family on that fateful night of the terrorist attack in Mumbai. I was in the theatre watching a movie when I got a frantic call that some firing was going on at Leopold Café, the family's restaurant on Colaba Causeway. I ran out of the theatre with conflicting thoughts of riots or gang wars crowding my head. As I neared our restaurant, I was horrified to hear the sounds of wailing and crying and witnessed a terrifying sight. There were injured people lying around; dead bodies being carried away.

I panicked! Where were my husband, my brother and my brother-in-law? I could not reach them on the phone; neither could I get into the restaurant. I cannot stand the sight of blood, it scares me, but it was my husband who was inside so I had to go in. The crowd however was holding me back thinking I was someone desperately running around looking for someone. They took me to the police station, pushed me in from one door but, in the ensuing frenzy, I ran out from the other exit. What was I to do? Where was I to go? What was happening?

I was totally lost. I called out to God as we all do in times of crisis. I was near the restaurant again and from somewhere I heard my husband Farzad's voice calling out to my brother. I have never felt such a deep sense of relief as I did on hearing him, but it lasted for only a few seconds. I immediately saw my brother walking towards me with his clothes all stained with blood. Had he also been shot at? Was he wounded and bleeding? 'No no,' he quickly assured me and hastened to add, 'keep away Shahnaz … it is a terrorist attack and I am just carrying the bodies. It is their blood on me.'

But how and where was Farzad? When the chaos eventually subsided, I found him at the Colaba police station and got to hear his side of the story.

At any given time, and especially on a day when the restaurant is full as it was that evening, you will see my brother-in-law Farhang standing near the entrance, helping customers get seated. My husband is always at a table near the counter. These were the two specific spots that bore the brunt of the attack by the terrorists. The first grenade was lobbed at the table where Farzad always sits. It blasted the poor couple that just happened to be standing there waiting to be seated. The second target was the other entrance to the restaurant. The people there were mowed down. The restaurant was in shambles.

So how was it that the men of the family were saved? It was because something that was seemingly insignificant, but totally unbelievable, had occurred. A few minutes before the attack took place, Farzad and Farhang had both gone up to the mezzanine floor to watch the cricket match being telecast between England and India.

Who or what made them go up together at that particular moment to watch the game? I can only think it was my God Meher Baba. I think – no, I don't think – I am 110% sure that if it hadn't been for Baba, they too would have been killed. It was His mercy, His compassion and His love for my family, and our faith in Him, that saved them both on that night.

How and why am I so sure? Because one more totally unbelievable thing happened. A couple of days after the attack, I got a frantic call from my cousin from New Jersey asking me, 'Shahnaz, who owns a Prado in Mumbai? Can you find out for me please?'

'You have been in a Prado a thousand times to Meherabad and you cannot recognise it? But why do you ask?' I countered.

'Because there is a picture of this car in the New York Times and it is being flashed everywhere in the world. But that is not all! There is also another fascinating picture peeping out of that car and everyone here is phoning up like mad to find out who that is. Go on the net and check it out for me please!'

I went to the computer and was totally amazed by what I saw. It was the picture of a car standing on a street just outside my restaurant that day. It had been damaged like many other vehicles in the vicinity. But this particular one was riddled by bullets and hit from all sides. The side windows, the roof, and

The picture of Meher Baba's face on the back windscreen of the car.

the windshield had all been shattered. All, that is, except for the rear windscreen, which is showing broken in only a few places. And there in the middle of the back windscreen is a clear picture, with not a single scratch on it. It is a picture of Meher Baba and it is my car!

Tears of immense gratitude rolled down my eyes. I knew without a shadow of doubt that it was Baba showing His love. But the true significance of it hit me a while later, when I began to look at the bigger picture and understood its deeper meaning. I know that many people, including other Baba lovers, must have lost their loved ones in this attack. We cannot explain why some are saved and others are not. Destiny or karma – who knows? It is not for us to judge. I am just so grateful that Baba's Grace was on us. Somewhere, somehow, this picture of my car and Meher Baba was brought into focus by an unknown photographer to show the world that, even in the worst of times and during the most horrible moments, Baba is standing by to help all humanity as much as possible and in whatever way He can.

Another story that gets across what I am trying to tell you will bear startling testimony to this.

Sevanti Parekh

The night of 26th November 2008 was the darkest in my life. It was that night that I lost my son Sunil and my daughter-in-law Reshma. They were both shot dead by terrorists in the Tiffin Restaurant of the Oberoi Hotel. Actually, they were not supposed to be dining there that night. Just two days prior to the attack, Sunil was scheduled to go to Japan. But at the last minute he just did not feel like going, and had cancelled his programme. So he had planned to have dinner with a friend at the Bombay Gym, but that also got cancelled and the venue was shifted to the Tiffin Restaurant. Destiny was playing its part, and the Divine plan was enacting it out.

Our world had fallen apart. I had never been a very religious person, I had no guru, and what little faith I had in God – I lost that as well after this tragic event. During our period of grief, a friend of mine gave me a book called *Sounds of Silence*. Since I was in no mood to read anything about gods, or spirits, or anything of that sort, I just put it aside. But I don't know what motivated me to pick it up after two or three days again and open its pages. I read the name of the author – Nan Umrigar – and it rang a bell. I had known her from my college days and, although we had not kept in close touch, we would meet once in a while. So I began to read it and found it so compelling that I could not put it down. I read about the tragedy that had befallen her when Karl died. I recalled that my own son had known Karl as both of them used to ride at the Amateur Riders Club.

I got in touch with Nan and met with her to talk about my loss. This meeting helped me in more ways than one, and what followed gave my wife and me a lot of hope and peace. Thanks to Nan and her book, we felt a strong desire to go to Meherabad. It was the first time I was visiting such a place and we set off on 31st January 2010 with some friends, not really knowing what to expect. We did not realise that this was a very special day and that it was the 'Amartithi' of Meher Baba – the day He dropped His body. We had read in the book that the hill on which the Samadhi stands is a very quiet place where you can roam around at will and find your peace with Meher Baba, but we were totally shocked to see that there were hordes of people there. That hill was so crowded; there was no place to stand, leave alone sit.

Actually we had reached quite late, I think it was about ten minutes before 7 pm. To have darshan at the Samadhi was just not possible as there was a long queue, and we thought we would not be able to enter the Samadhi and pay our respects to Baba that evening. So I was standing very dejected on one side, thinking that the whole trip is wasted when, lo and behold! A woman came up to me and asked, 'Are you Sevanti Parekh?' I said, 'Yes.' She was Havovi Dadachanji, one of Baba's old followers, who happened to be on Samadhi duty at that time. She said, 'Come on, I will take you' and led me right inside the Samadhi. For me this was nothing short of a miracle because I had given up all hopes of having Baba's darshan, and now here we were personally being led into the Samadhi. We stood there transfixed. I felt such deep peace and happiness; I felt loved!

Since that visit in 2010, three more incredible incidents have taken place.

It was my son's birthday on 17th July, and our office staff wanted to celebrate it, as they had been doing all these past years. On that day, we received a communication from Nan that mentioned two things. One: my son and daughter-in-law had said that 'through courtesy Meher Baba ... today you will receive ... we are sending you an international cake that's made with ingredients from all over the world.' It didn't make any sense to me at the time. The entire staff was assembled for the candle lighting ceremony at 3 o'clock in the afternoon when a delivery boy suddenly arrived carrying a box. We opened it and what do you think was inside? It was a cake! A cake from an international trading house, one of the largest trading companies in the world. The person who sent it may have been a friend of my son. I immediately realised this was one clear proof of what my son wanted to convey to me; that both of them are happy with Meher Baba; that they know exactly what is happening and wanted us to know it too.

But wait, there is more! The second surprise came when the candle was to be lit and, of course, the staff wanted me to light it, but I just couldn't. So, my daughter volunteered but even she kept hesitating. Then just before she touched the match to the box, the match flared and lit! Most of the staff gathered around also witnessed this phenomenon.

The third incident relates to the same message that had come that day through Nan. In it was a sentence at the end that said, 'Dad please, please feed some pigeons for me.' Now I know that my son loved birds and animals but I could not understand the significance of the message. I do know that there are *kabutarkhanas* where pigeons are fed in Mumbai, but I don't ever go there. But since he requested it, I told my wife and my daughter that maybe we will go somewhere and feed some pigeons. But where were we to go? Then I remembered that there is some temple in the Madhav Bagh area where my son's friend had put up a plaque bearing Sunil's name and renovated the place in his memory. This day being his birthday, this friend had requested that we go and do a puja there. I am a Jain, not a Hindu, but that didn't matter as, normally, I don't even go to Jain temples. So we accepted the invitation and went along with him to the temple. As soon as we went there and finished the puja, the father of my son's friend suddenly said, 'Would you please feed some pigeons for us?' And can you imagine, right before us there was this small place where there were pigeons clustered around, some grain kept ready to be scattered, and thus we fed the pigeons.

These three experiences sealed our faith that there is really somebody up there watching over all of us. This also did a great thing for me. I lost my biggest fear – the fear of death. We have lots of friends who are doing well and having such a great time that I always feared this was going to end one day. But now I realised that this life is only a journey; that after we complete it there is another spiritual world waiting for us and, therefore, there is nothing to fear. It is Meher Baba who is teaching me all this now.

I am also quite sure now that there is another world where we really belong. And I think all of us shouldn't ever worry about what is, and what is going to be. We should do our best while we are here in this world, and then prepare to move on.

CHAPTER 8

The Hand of God

My youngest sister, Dina, was born with a handicap. I lived with her for eighteen years, loving and cherishing every moment I spent with her. I remember her always smiling, sitting in the garden of our home in Mumbai, waiting for me to come home from school – to smother me with hugs and kisses. I would always bring something home for her: a pencil, a crayon, a book, some toffees or sweets. She loved going to the movies with the family and we all did most things together. She was a happy child, for my mother had opened a school for her at home and she was one of the brightest students who loved every minute she spent in it.

That school was visited by Jawaharlal Nehru once, who gave his blessings to it and to the work my mother was doing.

Former Prime Minister Jawaharlal Nehru photographed along with my mother at the school for children in need of special care.

The school is now relocated on Sewri Hill in Mumbai and is called 'The School for Children in Need of Special Care.' It now has nearly 800 children and a staff of 300 to look after their special needs. Recognised by the government as one of the best of its kind in Mumbai, it is now being managed by my elder sister, Tehmi Shroff.

So, one day when Rangoli came to meet me and told me about her very special child, I understood her needs perfectly and told her immediately about Baba.

Rangoli Dhingra

Ravi and I are the proud parents of little Rohan who was a 'special' child (I say 'are' because we will never, ever stop being his parents). Rohan suffered brain damage at birth due to the negligence of doctors. As a result, he became severely handicapped – he could neither talk, sit, stand, nor walk. He had a severe hearing loss and poor vision. In medical terminology, he was a 'Spastic with Cerebral Palsy'. But Rohan was truly a gift from God. He communicated with us through sight and touch. He was a beautiful baby and for the eleven years he was with us, we led a wonderfully happy life with him.

On 28th December 2009, we lost Rohan – suddenly, unexpectedly. While we always knew that Rohan would not live a normal span of life, we were not at all prepared for losing him so early and so suddenly. Ravi and I loved him dearly and for us he was our 'normal' child. His passing did not embitter us; we had no complaints against God. He fulfilled all that we asked of Him. I always prayed to God, that when Rohan goes, his going should be painless and peaceful. And God had listened to our prayer and granted our request. I had also prayed that he should go before I did and that was the way it had been.

On the morning of 28th December, Rohan got up normally and played with us in bed. That was his favorite time of the day when he had our undivided attention. We had had a late night and wanted to sleep some more, but Rohan was fresh and up at his usual time of 4 am. He played, laughed, gurgled and drooled – and kept urging us to get up. We had to finally give in to his playfulness. I went to the kitchen to soak his medicines while Ravi continued patting him with eyes closed; gradually his soft cooing stopped, and he went to sleep ... never to wake up again! There wasn't any struggle; no discomfort, no warning signs that he was going. At first we thought he must have been tired or suffered a minor seizure (which was not unusual). He would usually recover after a brief nap. It's only when we noticed his blue lips and nails that we became alarmed and rushed him to the hospital.

But it was too late. He was already gone! It troubled Ravi deeply that he did not do anything while his baby was going. He had not even come to know! The feeling that Rohan went away because we had upset him over something constantly haunted us. Had we hurt him in any way?

One by one, the rituals got over: Rohan's one night in the mortuary; his last journey to the crematorium; the immersion of his ashes in the sea. These are moments that will remain etched in our hearts, and in our memory. The puja on the fourth day, the prayer meeting on the thirteenth day, all went peacefully. The helpless feeling of being unable to hold on to time overcame us. It was as if with each passing day, our baby was going further and further away from us.

But silly little worries continued nagging me. He was a baby; we hadn't left him alone for a single day; he was unable to feed himself. Who would be feeding him? Who would be bathing and changing him? Rohan loved being dressed up three to four times a day. And that last puff of the baby powder always made him smile. Although he was challenged in so many ways, he knew that he wasn't completely ready until I ran a comb through his hair. He was indeed a beautiful child.

Sometime during the first month of Rohan being taken away from us, Dr. Asha Chitnis, a dear friend and Rohan's physiotherapist since he was five months old, gave me some books to read. Until then, I had never read any book on philosophy, religion or spirituality. Looking after our son and providing him with love, care and medical attention was the only path we followed. Of all the books that Asha sent, I picked up *Sounds of Silence*. The story was that of a mother who had lost her son and that was an instant connect for me. I finished reading it in one day. I could identify with every word, every line in the book. It wasn't fiction. It was a narration of a deep, personal loss of just the kind I had gone through. The last page of the book carried the author's email address and I was tempted to get in touch with her. I thought how wonderful it would be if I could somehow get in touch with Rohan and get to know his whereabouts. And if Nan could, then perhaps I could too. I wrote to her and in a few days she called back with a message from Rohan! Needless to say we were delighted and wanted to know more. She called back in a couple of days while on a visit to Mumbai. I desperately wanted to meet her and was hoping she would agree to come to our home ... Rohan's home. She did come and that day changed my life.

Nan Aunty spoke to me about Karl, whom I felt I already knew well through *Sounds of Silence,* and she spoke to me about Avatar Meher Baba whom I knew nothing about. She urged me to visit Baba's Samadhi in Ahmednagar, which I promised I would. Not because I felt the need to but because she convinced me it was the first step.

It is usually difficult to take time out from our schedule for any holiday, but somehow things worked out and within the next two weeks the trip to Meherabad materialised. For those of you who have read Nan's book, you will understand when I say that I went there looking for Rohan but was disappointed since I couldn't find him there in any form. But the serene environs at Meher Baba's Samadhi filled us with peace. Baba was new to us but obviously we were not new to Him. It was after this trip that I experienced Baba's presence in my life. The tightness in my chest and the sadness in my heart diminished. I could breathe easy. Baba did not work magic but He did give us great strength to deal with our grief.

When Nan Aunty had come to our house, she had asked me if I would like to communicate with my son. 'Oh yes!' I had said. I desperately wanted to know about my Rohan. Why did he go away so suddenly? Where is he? How is he? And, if at all he is upset with us for letting him go away without being able to do anything for him. So when she got us Baba's message through Karl, we were overwhelmed. My son could not hear or speak, and never learnt to read or write. He only communicated through his eyes and touch, and only understood the language of love! So there was this deep desire to exchange some sort of 'words' with him. I requested Nan Aunty to initiate me into auto writing. Rohan never went to school but I hoped that now he would learn to write and send me messages in the future.

Many may doubt the authenticity of Karl's message and may question my belief in auto writing, but I found my answers in the message itself. The fact that we could do nothing for our son while he quietly passed away was adding guilt to our grief.

Karl's first message from Baba eased our grief considerably. He had written, *'Rohan took on this very difficult journey for a reason. He chose his parents accordingly, and you have fulfilled every single need that he had. Baba sends you and your dear husband a lot of love and blessings for being the perfect instrument to further the journey of one who had chosen such a difficult life, and helped him to go through it with flying colors. God bless you both. Love, Karl.'*

On 28th February 2010, I started communicating through auto writing with Rohan. The initial scribbles, loops and wavy lines did not deter me at all. During this time I met Nan Aunty several times and each time my hope and faith got stronger. In the course of the following months, we came to meet a lot of wonderful people through Nan Aunty. People who were connected to Baba in some way or the other: Cyrus, Lisa, Jehangir, Priya, Aarti, Anil, Gautam, and many others touched our lives, and remain friends to date. Grief, as we realised, was not just for us alone but also afflicted many others who, like us, had arrived at Baba's doorstep.

Sometime in the month of March, we noticed the first words coming up in my writing with Rohan. He wrote the word 'bless' almost nineteen times one day, and repeated my maiden name 'Sood' several times. And then came 'bless Soods'. We assumed he was talking of his love for my parents and my family who loved him dearly and did everything possible to make him comfortable and happy in life. Soon words started connecting and before long he was writing small sentences. Each morning we looked forward to hearing from our baby and were overwhelmed by most of what he wrote. And now after more than a year-and-a-half of writing, Rohan sends us beautiful messages that help us to face each day with a smile. His messages are meant for us, but are universally applicable. Regarding our grief at losing him, he once wrote: 'Do not grieve for the branch that fell off the tree. It was a part of the tree, yes, but it is the same branch that falls on the ground and grows back again, this time as the grapevine. Notice that the grapevine goes round and round the tree, hugging it not once or twice but over and over again. And one day the entire tree is covered in the loving embrace of that grapevine.'

Many a times I have doubted the authenticity of Rohan's messages, often blaming my subconscious for what is written. But over and over again our baby has given us reasons enough to believe in him and what he has to say to us.

Last year we were to visit Pune for some work. A week prior to our departure, Rohan kept writing 'go', 'go', 'go bund', 'go bund'. We were new to Pune and couldn't figure it out what he was writing. But on the way to our place of work, we crossed a road called Bund Garden Road. We were delighted to see this but still couldn't figure out what was so special about this road. My brother, back home, tried to Google 'Bund' and came up with a connection between Avatar Meher Baba and Bund Garden Road. To our surprise and utter delight, we discovered the Guruprasad Meher Baba Memorial on Bund Garden Road. I immediately called Nan Aunty and she confirmed the same. Who would believe our baby would lead us to Baba in such a beautiful way!

Rohan endeared himself to anyone and everyone who laid eyes upon him. Yet there were some people who had the power to make me angry and arouse negative feelings in me. They were the ones who were most insensitive to his condition and wanted

The Meher Baba Guruprasad Memorial on Bund Garden Road, Pune

to move on in life, with or without him. Better still without him! Our hurt knew no bounds when Rohan's passing was treated with callousness by them. And that is when hurt, hatred, resentment, and a vow never to forgive them took root in my heart. These negative feelings simmered and started affecting my well-being. Rohan often guided me to 'forgive', to 'let go', but much as I tried I couldn't.

Early this year, Rohan started directing me to 'deep breathe' and 'rest'. Time and again, he would tell me to take care of myself. And then one day we discovered a nodule on my neck, which turned out to be cancerous. This devastating revelation should have shattered us but, surprisingly, we took it all so calmly. We often wondered where the strength to deal with something as ugly as cancer came from. We should have known. Subtly but surely, Beloved Baba was working his way into our lives. The diagnosis was worrisome, but I was thrilled. Not because of the illness, but because my son knew about it and was warning me too. I was confident that I would come out of this condition unscathed. The treatment began, the surgery went off well, I started recuperating and I spent the next few months doing exactly what my baby had recommended: 'deep breathing' and 'resting!' Around this time, my son insisted I get stronger from within. He wrote: 'Notice this … all construction, all-building up, all growth happens inside out. A pillar gains its strength not from the bricks, cement or plaster! What make it strong are the iron rods within. And a flower … it stands tall in full bloom not because of the stem or the leaves but for the network of roots inside the soil. Remember, strength lies within, it lies inside.'

My baby advised me to 'let go' and to 'accept the bitterness in my life,' or else no one would suffer but me. He wrote: 'Sometimes the bitterness can cure. Just like that bitter sugarcoated pill that the doctor prescribes. And if you must live with bitterness, grudges and grievances, so be it!! Only make sure you 'coat' it with 'sweetness'. Surround yourself with more peace, more happiness in life. You will see that the pill gets easier to swallow, does not leave a bitter taste in the mouth, and ultimately … cures.'

Day after day Rohan writes beautiful messages for us, addressing them all to 'mummy'! Ravi and I look forward to sitting together and reading our baby's messages every morning when I finish my writing. And one day, when Ravi pointed out that 'papa' was not mentioned in the messages as often as 'mummy', Rohan wrote: 'My Papa, you and I had silence between us. And to be able to share 'silence' is the greatest gift of all. Words speak and actions speak, but when silence speaks, it's the purest form of communication … for it is in silence that the heart speaks and the heart hears!'

It is true that God chooses to work through his people. Baba chose Karl and Aunty Nan for us. And as we surrender to His definite presence in our lives, who knows, one day, He may choose us for someone else?

So much about the baby, who very early in life, went to Baba. What about those who live to fight another day? Read what Delna Dhamodiwalla has to write …

Delna Dhamodiwalla

'Wonder Baby!'

That was the caption flashed on the front page of The Mid-Day of 11th June 2011. A beautiful picture of Ria was displayed with a brief write up calling her a 'Fighter'! That's exactly what my daughter Ria is and she taught me to be a fighter too; she imbued me with the will to never give up.

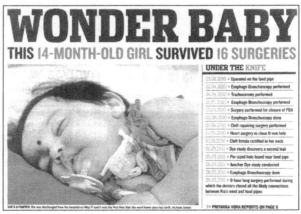

The photo of Ria published on the front page of Mid-Day.

Ria was born in Dubai on 21st February 2010. She had multiple congenital problems from birth for which she required surgery, but we never imagined she would have to undergo sixteen surgeries! She had been on the ventilator for seventeen months and confined to a PICU bed for fourteen months, which even the doctors believe is one of the longest stays ever for any baby they have ever treated, or even heard about. Her suffering was unbearable to watch. At first, the ordeal made my husband Jamshed and me very fearful and superstitious. We didn't know what we had done wrong to deserve so much pain and suffering.

It seemed Ria had come with a special agenda for herself, and for those coming in contact with her. Ria was a special child in more ways than one. She handled her first surgery of the Tracheo Esophageal Fistula, which lasted for five hours, on the second day of her birth.

Barely had she come out of that surgery, the doctors informed us that Ria had another very rare congenital problem, a Laryngeal Cleft – Type 2, wherein the food pipe and wind pipe remain conjoined with a slit in the throat. Dubai was not equipped with a Pediatric ENT Surgeon to perform such a surgery, so we had to fly to Lilavati Hospital in Mumbai. But before that main surgery could be done, Ria had to undergo two surgeries for Tracheotomy and Gastrostomy. As days passed, we continued to get one shock after another and I continued to pray to God to seek His forgiveness for any wrong my husband or I may have done.

24th April 2010 was a very special day for us. We were over the moon when after the surgery, we saw Ria for the very first time without a single tube on her face. She looked radiant, her smile heart-warming, and her face angelic. She had a special glow on her face that brought inner peace and calm to our hearts.

We thanked God but deep down we felt that not until God had forgiven us completely, would Ria come out safe and sound from the hospital. So to please God, I started going to church, making novenas, and sitting near the Blessed Sacrament and all that. Jamshed too was on an emotional roller coaster and began saying his prayers and visiting fire temples regularly.

But our joys were short-lived. On 26th April, Ria was diagnosed with acute fungal infection. My otherwise chubby, fair and pink-cheeked baby looked unusually pale and lifeless. The very thought of that sight sent a chill down my spine. I was fuming inside and charged out of the hospital and ran to the church ready to wage war against God. The mother in me shook the heavens above. At that time I was not aware that the infection had affected Ria's blood, liver, spleen, both the kidneys and lungs. I believed that God had the power to perform miracles and I was not going to leave Him without seeking my miracle. Just then Jammy phoned to call that this new doctor Dr. Uma Ali who had taken on Ria's case, had changed medicines and that Ria was responding well to them. I knew for sure now that God was there and He was taking care of her.

Returning to the hospital PICU from the church, I was surprised to see Ria blowing kisses. That's the way my little Angel is – magical! One moment she would desaturate – go low on oxygen, and the next she would be blowing kisses or smiling at everyone around. But the infection had gone deep and it took time for her to recover while we waited impatiently to get over with the main surgery and return to Dubai. Ria also had two heart conditions which also needed to be corrected but doctors said that since they were not life-threatening, they did not warrant attention at that point in time. Since Ria was not responding well to attempts to wean her off the ventilator, the doctors felt she needed to undergo the PDA closure to clip the extra artery in the heart for which she underwent a fourth surgery on 25th May 2010. She barely recovered from it when she had her fifth surgery on 7th June. A Laryngeal Cleft – Type 2 repair-surgery was done to separate the food pipe and wind pipe.

We now thought we were approaching the end of the dark tunnel, but were in for a rude shock when the doctors said that she would have to undergo another surgery since she was still dependent on high ventilator support. That we were feeling downright frustrated is understandable, but at this point, the doctors too felt the same. Left with no choice, the next surgery was done – an ASD Closure to close the 11 mm hole in the heart.

With this surgery, the ray of hope for Ria's survival became stronger. The God-sent Dr. Bharat Dalvi said there are 95% hopes that gradually Ria will wean off ventilators and the balance 5% is in God's hands. Initially, it was just the reverse and we felt that if God has supported us this far, He would surely attend to the remaining 5%.

With that hope we continued to pray and although Ria, because of her very low immunity levels, kept catching infections, we continued to stay at the hospital for months and months. Strangely, hospital seemed like home – we lived, ate, bathed, and slept there all the time. Friends, relatives and acquaintances kept visiting us and we also made many new friends. All the same, we yearned to be back home and start life afresh, but no doctor could tell us when that would be.

And this went on and on – surgery after surgery coupled with infection. Months rolled by and a time came when we were faced with a very difficult decision: Jammy's work and my seven-year-old son Zidane's schooling back in Dubai. In eleven years of married life I had never stayed away from them and it broke my heart when, on 29th October 2010, my pillars of strength had perforce to fly back to Dubai. At the airport, Jammy and I broke down but Zidane – I don't know where he got this understanding – wiped our tears and said, 'Don't worry, all will be fine.' He was calm, composed and confident. His faith was child-like; he made no demands of us and sacrificed a lot, knowing well that Ria needed us more.

The dawn of 2011 brought a ray of hope as the doctors talked about Ria's discharge, hopefully before her first birthday on 21st February 2011. As days went by, her ventilator settings were reduced, she needed only few hours at night, and doctors felt confident that she could be discharged if we had a full-time trained staff and a home paediatric ventilator. Sourcing both was a frustrating task. Ria turned one-year-old at the hospital. Doctors, nurses, hospital's office staff, friends, family and even the trustee of the hospital turned up. Cakes were cut, loads of gifts were given to Ria, and for that day we forgot that we were in the hospital. I was overwhelmed when the nurses pooled in to gift her beautiful gold earrings, and a cleaner got her a little dress.

When we were almost sure of a discharge, the doctors did a bronchoscopy just to be sure that all was well. Unfortunately they detected a leak somewhere along the food pipe, which required a nine-hour surgery to close all likely connection between the two pipes. She improved considerably after this.

At long last the day we had dreamt of arrived. On 17th April 2011, people gathered to offer loving goodbyes. As she was being taken home, the sight of flying birds, the sound of their chirpings, the touch of a gentle breeze caressing her cheeks and the honking of the cars – all new to her, lit her face as she started breathing fresh air for the first time in her life. How I wished my Jammy and Zizu were there with me.

Ah! Home, at last! Ria was progressing well and building up her immunity and weight. The house was maintained infection-free; it needed to be immaculately clean, and no visitors were allowed. Ria was finally weaned off the ventilator from 20th July 2011.

Looking back, I am convinced I could never have made it through all the trials and tribulations by myself. I felt a Divine and Pure Presence was guiding me inwardly. This made me stronger, more determined not to give up but go on without breaking down. And this Pure Divine Presence I finally recognised as that of Meher Baba whom I got introduced to when I was in the thick of the ordeal by the two earthly angels, Farzeen and Somit, who walked into our lives like the morning sun that dispels all darkness. They have been our single-most important source of support. They have been regularly visiting Ria and giving her the much needed healing light of Reiki.

I had many opportunities to go to Meherabad but I could not avail of them, as I could never leave Ria alone. But after reading Aunty Nan's books *Sounds of Silence* and *Listening to the Silence*, a strong urge to visit Meherabad arose within me. On 9th December 2011, in the company of Farzeen and her husband Somit and a few friends, I went to Baba's Samadhi. As I had left Ria in someone's care, and also the fact that we were planning to go back to Dubai, I wanted to know if Baba too willed the same for us. I now understood what it meant to surrender. I had asked Baba to show me a sign that He was happy with my decision, and that I should also be able to see a picture of his which I deeply connect with and, of course, to also meet Bhauji, Baba's only living male Mandali member. Baba accomplished these so beautifully for me. I cannot thank Him enough. As I entered the Samadhi, my heart was overflowing with Baba's Love. I felt light. Something deep down has changed within me. Today, I sincerely feel thankful to Baba for all that He has bestowed upon me: a kind, loving, and understanding husband, my children, my parents, my in-laws, friends, doctors, and nurses – and most importantly Ria, who brought me to my Lord of Love – Meher Baba.

As I had wished, we also got permission to meet Bhauji. We were told it would be brief, but that was fine with us. As we met him, he clapped on our hands thrice. We hesitatingly asked permission to click a photo with him to which he graciously agreed. For me it was as if Baba was giving His darshan, so I just wanted to hold on to Bhauji knowing Baba was there. Then I saw a photo of Baba, smiling as if talking to me, telling me that all will be fine and that He would always take care of us all.

At home, I wrote this for Baba and I hope Farzeen puts a tune to it so that, some day with my family and friends, we can all sing together at Baba's feet – glorifying Him and His love for us all!

'Now that I've found You nothing seems worthwhile
I'm drowned in Your love and Your beaming smile
You rescued me and brought me back to life!

Chorus: Baba You're my savior and You're Divine
You alone are the only one and You are mine

Through pain and suffering You made me strong
You gave me hope to carry on.
You showed me the way and guided me through
BABA …

You came into my life like the morning dew
Soft and gentle with sprinkles few
You held my hand in day and night
In my darkest hour You were by my side
BABA …

You showed me to love and be patient through
You taught me to forgive and be humble too
The fear within me You washed away
You filled my heart with love each day
BABA …

Life cannot be complete without You
You are the Creator and Lord too
You are my everything
Life revolves around You
I hold Your *daaman*
Just like a child would hold, You do.
BABA …

CHAPTER 9

The Pilgrim's Progress

'If understood, life is simply a jest,
If misunderstood, life becomes a pest,
Once overcome, life is ever at rest,
For Pilgrims on the path, life is a test,
When relinquished through Love, life is at its best.'[1]

Priya Pardiwalla and I have now been friends for many years. It all began one day when I approached her to design the cover of my first book *Sounds of Silence*. She read it through and called me, in tears as it was too emotional for her and she could not find it in herself to proceed with the work. However, she suggested a few titles out of which I chose – *Sounds of Silence*.

Since then she has been a close follower of Baba and loves Him dearly. Here is how she has progressed on the path...

Priya Pardiwalla

As we learn how to appreciate those experiences that we don't like as much as those we do like, life becomes more joyful and we become more free. Each one of us has had experiences we don't relish, or like to remember. Experiences that lead us to question this 'silent man in the sky' we call by different names. He is Jesus... Allah... Ram... Ahuramazda... Buddha... Krishna... and He is Baba.

Yes, I call Him Meher Baba for it is only He who has made me realise that sometimes life hands us lemons. The trick then is to turn them into lemonade; sit down quietly ... reflect ... sip the nectar ... and fully enjoy the experience!

Now, after coming to Baba, as I turn back and reflect upon my life thus far, somehow all the problems and difficulties seem to fade away and all I can remember are just the wonderful things that have happened to me – even though the trials and tests along this journey were so many.

I remember the quiet love and encouragement of a doting grandma who unsparingly loved me, even through those terrible exams and even worse scores in math!

I remember the positive energy of loving parents giving me the strength to overcome my painfully shy nature, and to lick my crippling stage fright!

I remember the patience of a dear teacher who stood holding my hand as I trembled and struggled to jump into a swimming pool!

I remember the simple acceptance of my parents when I announced a career-change halfway through a Degree course!

I remember the strong support of a loving father as I spent agonising hours battling a polio and meningitis attack in my adolescence!

I remember the warmth, love and faith my folks, friends and colleagues displayed once again as I lay paralysed below the waist in a Mumbai hospital for two months.

I remember the quick action, the positive energy, and the help my friends, bosses, colleagues and neighbours offered when my Dad passed on!

I remember the strangers who turned into dear friends, and my present friends, who stood by me like family when my mum collapsed and slipped into a coma!

I remember and thank the daily miracles we all tend to take for granted. The sunrise, my pets, my family of friends, a hot cup of coffee shared with a beloved, the rain that quenches a thirsty earth, a clean bed to sleep in, love of friends, a quiet moment by the sea, a visit to my mum in hospital when I finish work early.

Even just the simple joy when I see my mum open her eyes on a visit; the smell of freshly baked bread; the smell of popcorn in a movie theatre.

The streak of 'pink ribbon' seen in the sky from the window of the plane.

I remember the day that Steve and I were on our way to Goa for the Goafest Awards and had asked Karl for a sign. He had said that we will see him as a pink ribbon and then, just as the plane began its descent into Goa, I remember how it had blown our minds when my eyes flew open to see a brilliant streak of pink running like a single ribbon across the grey-blue sky.

But that is not all. Then an amazing thing happened. Steve and I were very anxious about the outcome of the function we had to attend. We had sent in a few entries from our team but not as many as we would have liked to due to constraints and lack of time. In advertising, as in most fields, an award means recognition of one's talent from the industry, and it also means a job at the end of the day.

Before we left for Goa from Mumbai on Thursday morning, I had asked Karl as usual. I guess he knew our inner turmoil and anxiety regarding the approaching awards festival. As he normally does, he reassured me of Baba's infinite love, support, and of His continued presence in our lives.

I cried on His shoulder telling Him about how competitive the industry is, and how a lot of professionals in the industry have godfathers and mentors overseeing and promoting them; about the lobbying and the social networking that happens and how all this decides the fate of a piece of work – whether it wins or not.

Karl asked us to put our faith in Baba and leave it to Him. And then I guess to cheer us up he said, *'I will be there with you as the big white bird sitting upon your shoulder, I will be the big, really big white bird. I will be there!'*

We landed in Goa early Friday morning and right from the start, Steve and I kept searching anxiously looking for signs of a big white bird that would alight and sit upon Steve's shoulder. There were none. Even at the festival we looked and looked, thinking maybe its a print on a tee shirt, a toy, a sticker, or even a tattoo, but we saw nothing. The day drew to a close. I started feeling both anxious and disappointed. I felt disappointed because we hadn't yet spotted Karl, and anxious because the award show was about to start in the next twenty minutes and, although we had two nominations, we didn't know if we would win!

Then as my whole group was sitting on the beach watching the para sailing and water bikes zooming around, I happened to look over Steve's shoulder ... and the most amazing sight met my eyes! There ... right there in the sky formed clearly above Steve's shoulder was this most amazing image of a huge, magnificent white bird! I pointed excitedly to Steve and then at the sky. We all rushed to the edge of the water in wonder and our hearts filled with hope as we saw this beautiful masterpiece that Karl had painted for us in the sky. It was lucky that we had our cameras with us so we could take this picture (as shown on the front cover of this book). It was Karl telling us 'I am with you my beloveds ... always, keep faith in Baba.'

Steve, I and our group went on to win both the nominations, winning two bronze medals. The beautiful white bird just melted away into the sunset sky.

Kim Verma Modi

The year was 2004. I used to talk to myself. I always felt like I was the only one who understood me. I didn't necessarily speak out loud; in fact, I rarely did. It was just things I would 'say in my head' and I always seemed to make 'me' feel better. But then one day I tried to listen ... really listen ... and the voice didn't sound exactly like me. It spoke of a world, a world beyond, full of love and happiness; a peaceful, cheerful place with no sickness, poverty or despair. Then after reading *Sounds of Silence*, about Karl and Nan's relationship, I was convinced the 'voices' I heard were those of my angels. Over a period of time, my angels helped me bridge the gap between myself and the Divine light that we also call God, and have given me guidance and the non-judgemental security I craved.

When asked frequently about how I came to be a Baba-lover, my immediate answer is – through Karl and Nan. Through them, Baba reached out to me when I was sixteen years old and, though I was wary and sceptical at first, He kept trying till I submitted to Him in July 2001.

I have often been told not to speak so freely about things that are 'private' and 'personal' and 'not spoken about'. I cannot understand why faith, respect, worship and love need to be hidden ... in fact, I believe we should be sharing our faith and beliefs with all those we love, and with all those we come in contact with. All anyone wants is to be happy, so why is it that so many are embarrassed or ashamed of their search for this happiness? Am I a flower child? A new-age hippie? A communist? Am I stark raving mad? No, I am none of these. It actually amuses me when people direct these comments to me, for no other reason than I currently believe that shocking people is the best way to get them to notice you. If they notice, they will question, and if they question, they too will find 'Baba'. I survive on the flow of love that is present between me and those around me, and if this flow is empowered even more by an increasing awareness of Baba, then I too am empowered, and so is each person I come in contact with.

As we go through this Spiritual Revolution, we are more and more drawn to Babas and Gurus, Sadhus and Masters. So much so, that the individual importance and credibility that is owed to God has been somewhat lost amidst the numerous manifestations of this God, and in the midst of our hurried search for answers. God, while still very much present in all our hearts and minds, has been replaced by a less humble approach now as we all come to terms with our own Divinity. I believe that the attempted dissection and rationalisation of this Divinity is the surest way to lose it, and the answers we so frequently search for externally are always present deep within ourselves.

Clairvoyants, astrologers, tarot card and palm readers are all channels for higher messages to reach our world. While the desire and temptation to approach these people with regards to our lives can often be immense, one must stop and question why they are denying their own connection with God, and handing over our power to other mere mortals to guide us. If one is to follow the premise that 'I am God, and God is Me,' then the belief in the Universal oneness is unarguable. Further, if we are all one then surely our 'messages' are actually our own Divine knowledge, our higher selves, guiding us towards a reunion with that oneness, and so the content of these messages is definitely known to us all at some level of consciousness.

Now Baba too is a manifestation of God and, so one might argue, no different to any of the other deities mankind chooses to worship. This is true and therefore my connection with Baba is not a connection with the man that lived, but with the essence of what He stood for; the Universal Message of Love. It is mystically heart-warming when one receives 'messages' from deceased relatives and friends, and when special coincidences grab our attention. But Baba is a lot more than this.

Life on this side of the veil is hard, and we often find ourselves hurrying against the boundaries that the unalterable state of time has set around us, encountering numerous choices, options and paths along which we can direct ourselves, towards what we see as our future. For every feeling and emotion there is a counter feeling or emotion. In order to fully appreciate the positive, one has to first understand the negative. If this duality did not exist, there would be no room for each individual's spiritual quest, and our world as we know it would cease to exist.

According to Paramahansa Yoganananda, 'Man cannot help having desires, but most human longings hamper fulfillment of the supreme desire. Until he wants and has God, man will continue to long for whatever else he believes will make him happy.'

It was this simple understanding, along with Meher Baba's writings, that lead me to examine all my personal desires, and what I learnt (and am still learning) is that all our desires, our wants, are manifested as a result of fear. Baba doesn't ask for one to pray, to sacrifice, or to suffer deprivation of any kind. Instead He encourages us to enjoy our earth lives to the fullest, being directed only by love and truth. As long as one's free will is the same as God's will, and we open ourselves up to the Universal source of energy that is Love, we will always be protected, nourished and harmonised.

I drive a lot of people crazy with my unconventional and what my father calls unorthodox beliefs. All I ask of any of you is that if I, or should someone like me, speak of angels and find joy in a world that is not confined by the norms of society, then please leave us be. I am no longer in search of fame or fortune, but instead the rare gifts that life as a free spirit brings to me.

I am still in awe of Nan and thank Baba so often for her presence in my life. Her silent yet unrelenting support encourages me to 'try my wings and fly' (Karl's words to me!), and I am never disappointed. With Baba's picture smiling over me, I still aim to connect with His energy during my meditations. I hear things and I feel things, but I have long given up trying to identify my 'angels' as people; their 'identities' are irrelevant; their 'identities' are one and the same. To me now, it is not so much a question of who is speaking, but who is listening ... and what lies beyond.

Sue Masters

One cold November morning, a slight pain at the base of my throat made me sit up and take notice. As my fingers crept cautiously over the spot, I began to feel a small, hard lump. A visit to my doctor resulted in tests but no real diagnosis was forthcoming. I lived in tension till a friend told me about Nan Umrigar and her connection with the spirit doctor, Dr. Lang, who had an outlet in Wales. As luck would have it, we both happened to be in London at the same time.

I have known Nan since my racing days. I was at the race-course that fateful day when Karl fell. He had ridden many horses for my stable and I remembered him with fondness. So, the next afternoon saw me ringing her doorbell. As we sat and talked about old times she told me a little about her connection with her son Karl in the spirit world, about his love for and connection with the Spiritual Master Meher Baba, and about her book *Sounds of Silence*. In the course of our conversation, we eventually came to the subject of George Chapman and the spirit doctor, Dr. Lang. Nan had already arranged a few appointments for a healing session with him for a group of people from India. I asked her if I could possibly go with her and did not know, till recently, that it was actually her husband Jimmy who gave up his appointment for me that day.

That visit was something I will never forget. Assuring me immediately that the cyst was not malignant, he asked my permission if he could perform a 'spirit operation' to remove it and then proceeded to do so in the most unusual way. He asked me to return after six months and, sure enough, much to the amazement of my doctors and me, it had totally disappeared. My husband Masoom and I have now visited George Chapman at Wales and have been helped a number of times. We have always found him loving, kind and concerned, and his help has been invaluable to us.

Since all this was connected with Karl and Meher Baba, I thought it only fit that I should pay a visit to the Samadhi with Nan. At first, I found it rather difficult to sing the aarti or bow down to a Master. So I just went in, paid my respects, gave my thanks, and walked out again. But I have to admit that what I experienced there that day has drawn me back again and again. Now, I bow down at the Samadhi not just out of thanks or respect, but because I want to. I have come to love Baba from the heart.

There have been many times when I have appealed to Him for help and support – at the time of my mother's death; for the happiness and welfare of my children; for the aches and pains of life that I suppose are all part of growing. Talking about aching bones, I have to tell you that I am a fitness freak and exercise on a regular basis. So for years, when I was in Pune, every day my car would follow a certain route that took me to the gym. I was thus cruising along on a day when I was feeling particularly low, when suddenly my eyes were drawn towards a pole at the side of the road where a small sign read 'Baba House'. I stopped the car and walked into the lane, and there stood the quaintest little cottage you ever laid eyes on. I rang the bell and saw through the white-latticed window, an old gentleman coming to open the door. 'Welcome to Baba's home,' he said. I walked past a hallway scattered with old photographs of Baba and His family, past an open well covered with wire mesh, and into a tiny little room – Baba's Room. It was a room filled with Baba's Divine Presence. In the room were relics of Baba – His pink coat, His slippers, little knick-knacks, His handwriting hanging on the wall, and a blood-stained stone which spoke loudly of desperate days. I sat there for a long time, reading, absorbing and assimilating every little detail. What I experienced that day has been instrumental in bringing me closer and closer to Baba.

In 1998, my husband developed rheumatoid arthritis. His condition deteriorated rapidly till it reached a point when his ankle completely packed up and he had to walk with a stick. None of the doctors we consulted were able to help, except by way of putting him on a massive dose of steroids, which only added to his weight and heart problem.

I eventually asked Karl for help. He said, *'Massage the painful part of the leg slowly every day, keeping Baba in mind all the while and then leave the rest to Him.'* So, I sat quietly thinking about Baba every day. One day a friend walked in and seeing Masoom hobbling along with a stick, she burst out, 'Arre! What is this? And why do you have to go all over the world looking for a cure when you have the best doctor specialising in Rheumatology at your doorstep?'

It is a wonder that Masoom agreed to see him and that visit changed everything. Not only was this doctor brilliant, but also kind, considerate, and ready to answer any question. Initially we had to see him every four to six weeks and, in a short time, Masoom felt definitely better. He was able to walk more easily and life began slowly to return to normal. I continued the massages. Then it so happened that one day, while I was sitting in the doctor's waiting room for our appointment, I suddenly spotted a big picture of Meher Baba in one of his glass cupboards. I couldn't believe it! I had been there so many times before and had not noticed it earlier. I couldn't wait to ask the doctor how come he had Baba's picture with him. I was astounded to hear that the doctor and his family were also Baba's devout, faithful followers and had been so for a very long time. Can you believe that we had travelled all over the world to get help for Masoom, and Baba had brought it right to our very doorstep!

It was a difficult time for me when Masoom had to undergo a second bypass surgery. I was with my husband and daughter in a foreign country and scared out of my wits. But I had Baba beside me. That is the time I realised more than ever what Baba meant to me. I felt that He was there by my side all the time, holding my hand – not just leaving me to struggle alone, but actually going through all the emotions of patience and tolerance with me. He was giving me the strength to bear it all; to trust and then be content to leave the final result to Him. All I can say now is, 'Thank you Baba for coming into my life and enriching it with Your Love.'

CHAPTER 10

When the Student is Ready

*'Know, O disciple that those who have passed through the
silence, and felt its peace, and retained its strength, they long
that you shall pass through it also. Therefore, in the Hall of
Learning, when he is capable of entering there, the disciple
will always find his Master.'*

*– Light On The Path and
Through the Gates of Gold,* Mabel Collins

It usually happens that only when one has faced, or is
facing, hardship and sorrow and has one's face against the wall,
that one reaches a state of total surrender: a 'Thy will be done'
situation when one welcomes the higher forces to take over one's
life. However, this is not always the case and there are many
who are ready, even without misery being a part of their lives.

Whatever the reason may be, as we read the stories of two
totally different women, we will realise that the Master is always
there waiting, ever so patiently, for the moment when the disciple
will turn towards him and allow him to enter his or her life.
Since we all have free will, a Master cannot enter forcibly.
He must wait till such time as the disciple is ready for the teaching.
And it matters not what form he takes: the truth is the same, no
matter which path is taken to seek it out and reach one's goal.

Geetika Deepen

March 31, 1992 …

I had landed in Kathmandu with my husband only a month ago. It was bitterly cold and my labour pains had begun around 5 am. I decided to wake up Deependra, my husband, who had been sleeping unaware of my pains that night.

He panicked as he didn't know driving back then, and our driver would only report for duty at 8.30 am. It was 'me' pacifying him, telling him everything will be alright … that I can drive myself to the nursing home … and I actually did! He managed to call the nursing home to tell them I was coming in, so they could arrange for the doctor to be there. To cut a long story short, within half-an-hour of being admitted, I delivered an adorable baby boy!

I was so grateful to God that everything went so perfectly and, all through, I strongly felt the presence of some power giving me the strength I needed. I closed my eyes in gratitude and instantly decided that I would name my son Mehar, as in 'meherbani' or God's blessing. The next day when we informed my parents in India that Mehar was born, my mom immediately responded, 'Great! Meher Baba has come!' I found it strange, but didn't pay any attention as to why she said it and later totally forgot her comment.

Fourteen years passed. During this time, we had moved from Kathmandu, travelled to the US and even stayed in Kolkata, Delhi and Chennai, as Deependra's job took him all over the globe, until we reached Pune in 2005.

One morning in 1998, my father passed away. There was no heart attack, illness, or hospitalisation involved. He bathed in the morning, sat to meditate, and never opened his eyes again! Even though my father had lived a most fulfilling life, his sudden passing shook me. I walked with him on his last journey to the crematorium. Though ladies of our caste don't generally go there, I went because I felt he would have liked me to be with him.

For several years, every night when I went to bed, the sight of my dad's calm, sleeping body would rise in my mind, and then the flames of the burning pyre completely dissolving his earthly form would trouble me a lot. Sometimes I felt that he was talking to me, but wasn't sure if this was true or just my imagination. Then one day, in Delhi, at one of Shiamak Davar's dance schools, I found a book called *The Laws of the Spirit World* by Khorshed Bhavnagri, in which she had spoken about her experiences of connecting with, and talking to, her two sons who had died in a car accident. I was amazed by her 'auto writing' method because, frankly speaking, I hadn't heard about it before. I wanted to meet her and ask if my dad wanted to connect with me, and if I could also be initiated into auto writing to connect with him.

I came to Mumbai that summer and went looking for Khorshed. I was told she had moved to Canada and that there was only Shiamak who could possibly help me. However, he didn't have time to see me for the next four months. Disappointed, I returned to Delhi. I read all their published books from Part I to Part V and started asking Dad, in my heart, to show me a way by which I could talk to him. Sometimes, I would sit with pen and paper and think of Dad, but I did not get any messages from him.

Seven years later, my son Mehar turned fourteen on 1st April 2009. We were in Pune then and he had invited his friends home for a party. The boys ran up and down the house creating quite a ruckus. In the middle of all that *hungama*, I received a call from my friend Suresh who was visiting Pune from Hong Kong. He asked if I could meet him somewhere for an hour or so. When I asked where he was, he said that he was precisely a lane away from my home! I insisted that he come over to bless my son and have cake with us. He was happy to do so. When he saw my son, he asked him his name and as my son said that his name was Mehar, my friend appeared to suddenly freeze. He hugged Mehar immediately and then, realising that the boy was feeling awkward, he shook hands and blessed him. He then made his way to our living room. As I arrived with a glass of water, I saw tears flowing down my friend's face. I sat beside him in silence for a few moments. He wiped his tears with his handkerchief and drank some water. As he smiled sheepishly, I insisted we talk about what was troubling him. He smiled and said that these were not tears of sorrow but of happiness, amazement and gratitude!

He told me that when he comes to Pune every year to meet his mother, he also visits the Samadhi and stays at Avatar Meher Baba's Pilgrim Centre at Meherabad, in Ahmednagar. But this time, due to his mother's sudden illness, he was not able to go there. It was his last day in Pune and he was on his way back to Hong Kong. He had woken up that morning feeling sad and guilty about not being able to spend some time at the Samadhi or at Meherabad. So he had spoken, in the depths of his heart, to Meher Baba and said, 'I always come to see You Baba, but this time because of my mother's illness I haven't been able to spend time with You. For once, can't You come to meet me?' And now at five in the evening when he had asked my son his name, and it was 'Mehar', he knew instantly that Baba had come to meet him.

I was amazed to hear this. It suddenly struck me that my mother, fourteen years earlier, had mentioned something about Meher Baba. I asked my friend more about Avatar Meher Baba. Now it was his turn to be surprised! He thought I must have named my son after Meher Baba. However, I had been quite unaware of this Being until this moment.

Suresh then gave me a number of a friend, Nan Umrigar, who was a Baba lover too. And he also narrated Karl's story in brief and told me how Nan had been connected to Karl through auto writing. My antennae went up immediately!

You see friends, how universal forces and our Higher Guides work? What followed is a journey I will always be grateful for. I met Nan, read her first book *Sounds of Silence*, and immediately felt a connection. I felt so drawn to Karl, Nan and Meher Baba. I met her often and found out my Dad was with Meher Baba too! I requested her to initiate me into auto writing, which she did.

Before initiating me, she suggested a visit to Meherabad. I accompanied her for the first time in July 2005. The sky was overcast and dark, the rain pelting down. We had hired a bus along with ten other people that Nan was taking there. On the way, I sat silently throughout, listening to others talk about why they were making this visit. They were all troubled, sad and seeking answers but I didn't have any questions for which answers were required and nor was I unhappy. I tried to think of a question to ask Baba when I reached the Samadhi, but nothing came to mind. I just spoke to Baba from my heart telling Him I had no particular question and just wanted to meet Him, be with Him, and get to know more about Him.

As we reached the Centre and walked towards the reception, I saw a plaque on a wooden stand outside the Dining Hall with Meher Baba's picture and the words, *'I may give you more, much more than you expect or maybe nothing, and that nothing may prove to be everything. So I say, come with open hearts to receive much, or nothing from the Divine Beloved ...'*

I also have a habit of becoming completely quiet when I'm looking at something beautiful; standing by the sea; when I'm touched by something; or, when I'm having a spiritual experience. I used to wonder how people could describe their feelings so eloquently as I always felt at a loss for words in such deep emotional situations. But this was also taken care of when we climbed up the hill to the Samadhi. We stood in line for Baba's darshan. It was raining; the trees all around were swaying with the wind; a few dogs, goats and cats were all standing under a shelter. It was all so peaceful. Just then I turned around and my eyes fell on another plaque outside Baba's Samadhi, which had Baba's picture with a finger pressed on his lips and it read, *'Things that are real are given and received in Silence.'*

You must have heard the saying, 'When the student is ready, the Master appears.' But I understood the true meaning of this saying only that day in 2005.

The teacher, the Master, the Guru is always there for you, near you, guiding you from within. Then comes one 'defining moment' in a person's lifetime when we notice and discover the Master's presence and understand His ways of working on our lives. I am overwhelmed with Baba's Love and feel so humble that Baba has chosen me to accept His love and spread His name.

Namrata Sachdev

I chanced upon *Sounds of Silence* two years ago when I was looking for another book in a similar genre, and the librarian recommended this one to me. It was a time in my life when I was seeking answers to a certain situation and as I read the book it touched my heart deeply – the author's grief was real and so too was the resolution of the grief. I mentioned the book and the place called Meherabad to my mother who connected it immediately to an article she had read some twenty years ago. We decided to visit Meherabad. We spent just one day there and found it was a nice, pleasant place; however, it appeared to have made a deeper impact on my mother.

At this point, I'd like to give you some background on my, should I say, non-existent spiritual side. I had been an agnostic for several years. Ever since I could think for myself, I questioned every tradition, ritual etc. Most of all, I disdained the worship of mortal beings and elevating them to the status of God. Over time, I had arrived at the conclusion that God existed, but I could relate to God only in an abstract way, not in any form or as some deity.

A month after my Meherabad visit, I had a strange dream. I saw that it's 1st February and a chat window pops up on my computer. As I open the chat window, I realise with a shock that the sender of the message is Meher Baba. The instant I read the message, it sends a jolt through me and I'm saying to myself, 'Oh my God! It's true! This is how Meher Baba sends messages!' While I don't actually remember the contents of the message, four words remained in my memory: Box, Hat, Sunglasses, and Gloves. Something about the message woke me up. I kept repeating the four words in an effort to remember them the next morning. I mulled over the words for the next few days, but there seemed to be no logic whatsoever to the words 'box, hat, sunglasses, gloves'.

Finally, curiosity got the better of me and I wrote to Nan Aunty to help me understand this strange message. The reply I got was quite unexpected and explained that in a previous life I had often travelled to meet Meher Baba. This message being flashed now to me was just to remind me of the days when I took my box, hat, sunglasses, gloves, and went so often and so happily to make the journey to Him. This reply generated an equally unexpected response in me as my scepticism came to the forefront and made me question Karl's message. Was this message for real? Was I being drawn into some kind of a spiritual cult? On the one hand, I wanted to believe and, on the other hand, I was sceptical. The only thing that rang a bell was that I have always jokingly told my mother that in some lifetime I must have certainly been British. Could this have been my last lifetime and the one in which I chose to visit Meher Baba?

Several months passed, and having tried various alternative avenues, I once again turned to Karl for some answers. This time, he asked me to be patient and advised me to think good, feel good, and do good as it would help me in the long run. From then on, I started to observe my thoughts, feelings, and actions, as far as it was possible to do. Thus, I embarked on a whole new journey. Beautiful insights followed. I started to understand how judgemental we are in every relationship in our lives; how these judgements create energy patterns that drain us and the other person; and how to, slowly but surely, release this negativity.

Though there were many unresolved questions in my mind pertaining to Meher Baba and while I was far from being a devout follower, I still wasn't able to completely put Him aside. Slowly, like a jigsaw puzzle starts to come together, I had begun to ask myself questions that really mattered. Do I like the overall teachings and philosophies of Meher Baba? Does this path help me become a better person? Am I more at peace with myself and with others around me?

One day, a thought struck me out of the blue: If you can see 'Me' in all other forms and things, isn't it odd that you cannot see Me in the most obvious, visible and expressive form – in people? The absurdity of the situation began to dawn on me and here are some thoughts that came to me ...

God appears in different forms to different beings. For some, He is the universal energy in all life forms. For others, He takes the form of a saint. To deny God's existence in either form means missing out on the very essence of His presence in everything and everyone. Some find it easier to see, believe and reach out to God through one form or being, while others see God in a larger, universal state.

One day, my aunt who was aware that we had visited Meherabad, informed my mom that on the twelfth day of every month, there is a ritual that is performed there. My mother impulsively said 'let's go' and I agreed even more readily. We weren't too far away from the date and we packed and reached there just in time for a late lunch. Over lunch, I commented that from the moment we decided to come here, everything had happened so fast: the tickets, the travel, and then, soon enough, we were there. At the same time, a similar thought had struck both of us: this time Baba has called us here!

The instant I closed my eyes while sitting in Baba's cabin, I felt a wonderful peace within me and slipped into a deep meditation. It was as if I could feel calming vibrations pulsating within the cabin. I had my answer: the energy circles are purer, stronger, and more powerful at the core, the centre of a spiritual place.

After this visit, I wrote again to Nan Aunty to ask Karl for help on a personal front and the answer I received was most unexpected. Karl said that my wish should have been fulfilled and it was surprising that it had not yet materialised. He then asked me to connect with Baba on a daily basis. The second part of Karl's message about connecting to Baba on a daily basis was something new to me, and I wasn't sure I'd be able to carry it out. The journey so far had certainly been insightful and beautiful but could I alter my thinking completely, and bow with all my heart? I decided to be honest and write back to Nan Aunty letting her and Karl know that it was all very well for me to like Baba's teachings and follow His path, but when I closed my eyes and prayed I could only pray to an omnipresent God. In my own mind I thought I had taken Karl's advice of thinking, feeling and doing good. I had, to the best of my ability, brought earnestness to my spiritual journey. Karl's reply put me at ease. He assured me that prayers and rituals are not really required. The idea of a Divine Presence was enough, and Baba was pleased with my sensible approach. I was on the right path. I felt so deeply reassured by that and now I find it so much easier to include Baba in my prayers.

When Nan Aunty asked me to contribute my experience for her new book, I wondered what I'd write. I had no remarkable experiences to gush over; just a simple journey beginning with doubts and resistance that was giving way to some measure of faith. That I had no definitions to describe Baba except say that, somewhere along the way, in Him and through Him, I found an ally, an anchor, an awareness of peace within me; a spiritual delight that I am experiencing for the first time.

CHAPTER 11

All are One

Ranjana Salvi

It is 1978. Mumbai's racecourse is buzzing with only one name – Karl Umrigar, the rising star on the Indian horse racing scene. I did not understand anything about races, but I do remember being irresistibly drawn to a small, enthusiastic, smiling figure on a horse, and blindly following everyone to the tote window to bet on Karl.

We had just been transferred from Calcutta to Mumbai, and I was expecting my first baby. We met up with some old friends who dragged us to the races every weekend. Sometimes, I even went wearing a maternity gown! My baby came in March 1979 and I stopped going to the races for the next twenty-three years. However, I do remember following the fortunes of this young boy Karl, and was saddened the day he fell on 15th April 1979. I could not get over it for days and lost total faith in the goodness of God. But then I got immersed in having my second baby and there was no time to think about much else.

It was much later that my spiritual journey actually started. In 1993, I was drawn to Reiki, Vipassana meditation and various other spiritual practices like Pranic Healing, Tai chi, Art of Living, Yoga, etc. But somewhere, something was still missing. Idol worship and rituals did not appeal to me. I tried to imbibe the family tradition by creating an altar in my own home but could not bring myself to perform the daily rituals. I also visited a lot of religious places and temples but somehow nothing appealed to me.

Around 1996-97, I saw an advertisement regarding the book *Sounds of Silence* written by Nan Umrigar. It said that the book was about how Nan communicated with her son, Karl, who had passed on. The name of Karl Umrigar jerked my memory and I purchased the book. I read it with keen interest and was strongly influenced with its content.

Sometime in 2000, I was feeling really low because my mother was not keeping good health and everything seemed to be going wrong in my life. I contacted Nan and got a few messages from Karl that helped me a lot. Some of the messages, which Karl sent me from the spirit world, were so specific, especially with regard to my mother, that I was left with absolutely no doubt that they were for real. As time went by, my communication with Karl through his mother increased, and my pull towards Karl grew stronger. I kept wondering why I felt so deeply about him till, one day, I could not resist asking him: 'Karl, what is it that drew me to the racecourse every weekend when you were at the peak of your career? What was it?'

Karl wrote back: *'Dear Ranjana, you and I have been and always will be good friends ... Yes you have also helped me many times and I know you always will. I have a debt to repay, not because I have to but because I want to. You have a kind heart ...'*

I cried. I thought that maybe everyone we currently know, every chance encounter we have, is probably due to some connection from the past. The exchange of communication with Karl was a tremendous learning experience. It helped me understand that Karl, Nan, my mother, I, my friends, your friends, her brother, his sister, my husband ... somewhere, somehow we are all connected one way or the other.

I had never heard the name of Meher Baba before. Who was He and where did He fit into all this? The first time I came to know about Him was while reading *Sounds of Silence* in which He was called a Spiritual Master and an Avatar. Then as luck would have it, I met Nan for the first time at a ladies' meeting where she had been invited to talk about her book and, there again, I heard more about Meher Baba and somehow felt drawn to Him.

I made my first trip to Baba's Samadhi with Nan and the others in July 2000. Nan had called and said that she planned to take a group to Meherabad. I felt a strong urge to go with her so I promptly agreed to go along. Karl sent a communication that

Baba would come to me in Meherabad, talk to me in 'Silence' and that I would understand, for it would be in 'the language of the heart.'

When we reached Meherabad, the beauty and calm of the Samadhi overwhelmed me. I was able to sit inside the Samadhi hall for some time during the earlier part of the evening and, by the time the evening aarti was over, I was so engulfed with love that I just broke down and sobbed. It had been years since I had sobbed like this, and I did not even have a reason to cry. I was experiencing a kind of deep love within me, and feeling extremely uplifted. Much later, I was told that this crying that I had experienced was a form of deep cleansing.

Since then, I have been drawn back umpteen times to Meherabad. The silence, the high-energy levels that I experience there have always left me feeling very peaceful and calm. One always comes back from the Samadhi with one's batteries charged, ready to handle whatever may lie ahead. Hearing about Baba's stories and reading His various books have answered all the questions I had for so long. The main learning being that I did not have to follow rituals and traditions to be one with God. Real worship is from within – from inside the heart – not in the outward muttering of words. As Karl had once communicated to me: *'Baba truly awakened me – He truly spoke to me in Silence – that was the language of the heart.'*

Life went on. I did a couple of courses in Personal Counselling as well as several levels of Clinical Hypnotherapy. My children were set in their careers, they got married, and my son went abroad with his wife. I had started my practice in my son's empty bedroom. I began having regular Baba meetings in our home. Nan would also come from Pune with her newfound Baba friends and we would meet as one big family.

Circumstances suddenly changed and a day came when I had to leave my lovely home to shift to a new city. My husband chose Pune. My friends, my family, everyone I knew and loved, were in Mumbai. I didn't like being in Pune. The flat we were living in was small compared to my big house in Mumbai. I had no friends in Pune and although I tried hard to adjust, I still felt miserable. While I was busy lamenting, Baba was making things happen for me, slowly and silently, which I was at first unable to comprehend.

It went on like this for almost three years. At last, a day came when we were able to finally sell our Mumbai house and shift into a bigger flat in Pune. After we had settled in, the very first thing I did was to call Nan and my Baba friends for a session at my new home. The first thing Nan said as she looked around was, 'Oh Ranjana, it looks exactly like your Mumbai home. It is so open and big and beautiful, and so is the ambience.'

I am now at peace. How can I not be when everything that He is organising around me is so positively good? I have all that I ever wanted: a beautiful home, which according to the games Baba plays with us has an identical layout to our Mumbai house, and two beautiful grandchildren. I also have my own clinic in the complex where we stay.

Through all these experiences and the numerous exchanges I have had with Karl where he revealed that in one lifetime I was his friend, and in another life his older sister, I have come to realise that death is not the end of life. I have learnt that as long as I stay connected with Baba, everything will keep going fine for me. He has proved it to me over and over again. Now, I understand Baba's silent teaching that the purpose and goal of spiritual awakening and spirituality is to learn to consciously, intentionally and unconditionally love and forgive each other.

As Baba says: *'You and I are not we, but One.'*[1]

CHAPTER 12

A Sign from Above

When I started this book, I had vowed that I would not come back to tell you more stories about all the signs that had been received from Baba; that I would avoid talking about that at all costs. Enough had already been written and said about the wondrous ways in which Baba showed Himself to those who longed for a glimpse of His love.

But, since my last book *Listening to the Silence* was published, I continue to receive so many letters asking for more that I just do not feel it is fair to keep it all to myself. So here are a few more instances of how Baba has touched the lives of different people, but this time they are not just confined to Mumbai and Pune. They have flowed to me from the remotest corners of the world – from Iran, Gangtok, Delhi, Mohali, Ladakh, Shirdi, and from even as far off as Russia. Some of these stories have been written in their own language and then been translated into English. We have tried our best to retain their original essence and flavour so that the meaning does not get diluted or lost in translation.

Whenever it would be nearing Xmas or New Year's Eve, I would miss my husband and children. Thoughts of those days when all of us were together enjoying the festivities would flood my mind.

It was during one of these moments that I opened my computer. A mail from Delhi caught my eye. It was from Tushar Kohli, the son of a friend of my sister. He would often email me for messages from Baba. This is what he wrote …

Dear Nan,

I have something that I thought you would like; something I thought to share with you on New Year's Day. I was going through my books yesterday and guess what I found? I found a schoolbook of Karl's when he was in Standard 10! I am scanning the cover and sending it to you because it has his writing on it.

Please see the attached file. I guess that his cousin Navroze must have got it passed down from him, and I got it from Navroze.

It surely is a Happy New Year for me to see this today.

Love and regards,

Tushar

Karl as a young boy.

The cover of Karl's school book.

One such story is that of Rohinton Mistry who was desperately seeking a job. His applications to different companies had yielded no positive results and, in desperation, he had finally appealed to Baba to help him find a good job. A few days after this, I was happily surprised to receive a mail from him. This is what he had to say ...

105

Rohinton Mistry

Jai Baba, Nan Aunty,

This is to inform you that I've finally got a job and will be joining ship on the 25th of this month. I want to thank you for the messages, and also thank Karl and Beloved Baba for their help. I am joining an Iranian cargo ship soon.

One interesting aspect, or whatever you may call it, is that when I was waiting in the sitting room of my company, I saw a horse racing trophy named 'The Karl Umrigar Trophy – 2008-2009. It has obviously been given to the owner of my company, Capt. N. Vasvani. I know now that I will be safe, and able to complete my contract. I am the only Indian on the ship – all the others are Iranians.

Thank you once again, and if there are any instructions from Karl or Baba, please let me know.

In His name and Love, Jai Baba.

12th June 2011. Today, I got a heartrending letter from Varsha – a mother in Mohali. Her younger son had passed away in his sleep and the family was in deep shock and despair. As soon as the mandatory ninety days were over, a message went a long way to help them come to terms with his passing.

But then her elder son, stationed in the USA, wrote to ask me for a message from his brother. He was also touched with the contents but, as it often happens, he needed some kind of proof that he was actually speaking to his brother, and no one else. I apologised to him for my oversight in getting the required proof, but gave him an assurance that Baba would surely find a way of convincing him in some way or the other. I must say he was extremely polite and assured me that he totally understood. I felt relieved.

A few days later, I was surprised to get another letter from him. I am reproducing the contents for you the way they came to me.

Parniet Singh

Subject: Re: Baba

Dear Nan,

I don't mind any question. In fact, I had encountered 2 incidents in last few days. I was in Ladakh for last 10 days and when I was visiting one of the monasteries I prayed to Baba for showing me that Sukham is with me, as he was supposed to be on this trip with me. When I reached the top, a black raven flew and came next to me. Was it Sukham?

I asked Baba for confirmation and when I went to a café, which I had been visiting for last few days, I was going through the books in the closet for reading. Suddenly, Meher Baba's book *The Everything and the Nothing* caught my eye. I sat there for the next couple of hours and went through that book. It was a great experience encountering these incidents at this moment. It did a lot for me.

Please thank Karl, and our family's gratitude to Baba.

Regards,

Parniet

One evening, Zainab Durazi from Iran, and her sister from Pune, came to share a cup of tea with me. Zainab did not speak a word of English, so it was her sister who explained the situation to me.

Zainab Durazi

Zainab's only son passed away under strange circumstances in Iran and, naturally, she was heartbroken. She kept saying, 'If he loved me enough, he would not have gone this way … Why? Why? Why?' It so happened that, very soon, she began receiving intuitive messages from him and, to her surprise and delight, most of them turned out to be true.

Time went on, until one day her son told her that she should go to Pune and there look for a lady who would help her to get closer to him. Just how she was going to do that was beyond her understanding but, since she had a sister living in Pune, she took the opportunity and came. She was actually in her sister's home narrating this strange story when, by some chance, Karl's very good friend, Homi Dhunjibhoy, just happened to be there. He heard it and blurted out, 'I know the lady – it must be Nanny Aunty that you have to meet and I will arrange it for you.' And so he did. At this point I wish to stress that, actually, Homi Dhunjibhoy did not just happen to be there. This was no coincidence. When a Master wishes to help a soul, the smallest events are planned, and are part of a much larger picture. Souls are used to help other souls in the most incredible manner.

I tried to tell Zainab about Karl as best I could – about his passing, about the writing, and how I had received so much solace and comfort after going to Meher Baba's Samadhi. Zainab thought about this deeply and then asked me if I could possibly get her a message from her son, which of course I agreed to do. The next day the message from her son came through Karl, and it was one of the most beautiful messages I have ever received. It had so much meaning, so much truth and beauty that I have to share it with you. I am sharing a part of the message I received with you:

'Mem (M'am)

People say that God is in heaven – and that is really true because now I see Him every day. I needed you to go to Pune so that Aunty could help you know about Him and help you to come closer to Him. I want you to feel His energy in your heart the way I do. Only going to Him will give you the understanding of why and what happened, and the peace that you desire will only come from Him.

Mummy I do love you – you know that very well. You and I share a common bond, which gives us access to each other in a way that no one else can understand. Mum please pray for me. I need you to do so. A Mother's prayer can help me more than anything else, so Mummy please do try. Make a contact with Baba. He will do anything for those who genuinely need it. I do need you to do what I have asked of you and I know that you will.

Love to you.'

Zainab went to Meherabad to say her 'Mother's Prayer'. She spent a few hours at the Samadhi beseeching Baba to help her son's progress into his next life. Then she had a heart-to-heart talk with her boy there, and came back to Pune a different person. She then came to see me, full of smiles, took pictures of all of us together to take with her, and flew home the very next day. This transformation, and the way it took place, always remains a marvel to me. I have seen it happen over and over again. Her son's telepathic message to her in Iran, her ready compliance to his wishes, her so-called chance meeting with Homi, her interaction with me and getting to know about Meher Baba, her trip to the Samadhi, the beginning of her communication with her son, and all this culminating in a deep and abiding love for the one responsible for it all – Meher Baba. Do you find that so hard to believe? This is what we know as synchronicity. It occurs all the time with so many of us, but the question is: are we aware of it? Constantly aware of how beautifully we are being guided and looked after?

Would it also be hard to believe, if I told you, that just as I was writing this all down, I got a call from Zainab in Iran to tell me that, just as her son promised, she is now getting beautiful and meaningful messages from him. She is thrilled to see how positively her husband has reacted to this and how happy she is that she listened to the voice that came from the silence of her heart.

Aparna Chalke

Dear Nan … this is something that you must know. All this while I was asking you if Karl must have taken my husband to Baba, you, of course, were kind and patient enough to soothe my feelings, asking me to have faith and trust.

Something spectacular happened the other day. My daughter is seventeen and goes to Khalsa College in Matunga, Mumbai. On the 18th of February, she was standing at a phone shop near her college to get her mobile refilled. This shop also doubles up as a STD/ISD phone booth. Now, an old couple of some foreign origin (maybe British, my daughter is not sure) came and wanted to make a call to their son in the UK. As fate would have it, the phone booth was not working at that moment. Since there was no other booth in the vicinity, they asked my daughter if she would let them make a call on her cell. She readily agreed to their request, and guess what?

The couple called their son 'Karl' back home and told him that 'they have reached'. My daughter had such an overwhelming feeling, that she kissed the couple. This to me is a perfect example of 'Karl-ism' and, together with Meher Baba, they wanted to drop me a hint that Kumar has reached them. Thanks everyone and love you all.

Love, Aparna.

Mikhail Zheltikov

At seventeen, after a grand High School graduation ceremony and the awarding of a diploma in June 1985, I left the school building and walked homewards consumed by one question: What's next? How and where do I take the next step in life? Sometime later, I had a peculiar experience. I felt some sort of energy force stop me at the crossroads and I lost all sense of my physical body, except for the crown of my head, where I felt a funnel of indescribable energy that permeated all through me and appeared to be unending. Suddenly, I heard a voice that I couldn't recognise as my own that came from within my head. It sounded like a thousand Tibetan trumpets and, at the same time, it was full of love and bliss: 'You can go wherever you want and do what you want, all directions are open to you, the time will come when I will call you and we will change this world.'

This experience was so profound that all questions and worries, doubts and disappointments, were swept away. Then I almost flew home to start my new life, a new stage of maturity.

Many years passed. I went to study at medical school, joined the army, got married, and soon after our son was born. I went on to become a successful businessman and almost forgot about my experiences as a youth. However, over the years I continued and deepened my yoga, Tai Dzi and meditation. One day in 1994, my old friend Alexander asked me to read the *Science and Religion* journal in which there was an article about an Indian mystic called Osho (Rajneesh). While reading excerpts from the conversation of the mystic, something happened. The thought struck me that this is what I've always been looking for. My friend did not deny it came from a book titled *Mustard Seed*, about the parables of Jesus. Initially, the book sunk in very slowly and with almost every sentence all my ideas about life were turned upside down. Its energy captivated me.

On 29th October 1995, an unexpected event occurred. My wife, Valeria, left the house on Sunday morning and never returned. A few days after her disappearance, when I realised what had happened, I fell into a state of utter despair. I fell to my knees and asked God for the first time directly, weeping, begging Him not to take her from me. Why was this happening to me? Further searches only helped to tighten the knot of helplessness and futility. After visiting one of the psychics, who told me the terrible story of her passing, I was unable to stop crying for hours!

While investigating her disappearance, we did not find any clues. Everything was mixed up in my head, I was completely overcome and exhausted, I had not had a chance to sleep. At some point, I just shut down and had this vision ...

I'm on the streets of my childhood days and my friend Nicolay is behind me. I am pushing the pram in which my son Anton is sitting. Suddenly I notice a small puppy running towards me wagging his tail. As he clings to my legs, I reach down to pet him and hear him telling me, 'Take me with you!' Surprised at hearing the pup speak, I quickly withdraw my hand and look back at my friend: 'Did you hear that?' I ask. 'No, I did not hear anything,' answers Nicolay. The pup hops in front of us. Suddenly, a big black crow swoops down on him and begins to peck at his eyes. Jumping up, I swing a leg to ward off the crow and, at this point, some unseen force grabs me like a feather and carries me upwards. I catch my breath. Almost instantly, the force puts me down on the roof of a two-storey house and then gently lowers me to the ground. A few metres away, in front of me sits a huge, sparrow-like faced man with big black eyes! He does not utter a word. I look into his eyes and through eye contact I first feel the deepest penetration into the consciousness of my being to its source in the navel (what is called the *hara*). At this point, there is a vibration that is perceived by me as 'OM' and with it I feel infinite power and bliss.

As I snap out of my vision, an overwhelming flow of energy wells up within me and I jump, unable to contain the joy and sense of freedom that fills me. Suddenly I feel free, confident and inspired. I feel some power is helping me from above.

I felt and realised that this was the 'Call,' the call of the beyond, and I began to feel some very subtle presence, which did not exist before. I understood that this Being, as I saw it in the form of a sparrow, was my teacher or guide, and that he shared his experience of compassion and love with me, at the right time and right place. But who was he?

My life began to change. I started reading about and studying various spiritual traditions. My dreams became more aware and connected. I often foresaw events in great detail. During this time, in my astral dreams, I was often still in a school where I had mentors and a different kind of training and testing in non-identification with fears and limitations of my mind.

At other times, my dreams or visions were so clear and unpredictable that I could not tell where the dream ended and reality began. As all this continued to happen, what I began to experience was infinitely more than any experience tying me to the rough world of material reality. And from that time onward, the line separating me from my dream and reality got completely dissolved.

In November 2000, I first came to India. I had no knowledge of the language, no clear plan; just a fierce determination to find the Master who existed within me. I went with some Russian tourists, who were on the plane with me, to the *ashram* of Satya Sai Baba. I was there for three days but did not feel any connection. Then I came to Pune to the ashram of Osho, where I met some very interesting people, who were well-advanced in meditation and awareness, and some of them became my temporary teachers. I took *sanyas* and received the spiritual name of Swami Nirav Yakiz, which means 'Aware Silence'.

After several months in Pune where I lived through many important experiences, I went to the Himalayas. At Kathmandu in Nepal, I got acquainted with Elana, a girl from England. I felt a close connection between us and began to share with her whatever was possible in the direction of a spiritual search. We went to Russia together and I took her to many places of spiritual importance. Eighteen months later, we returned to India and had an opportunity to be part of the resident programme in the ashram of Osho. We worked for the benefit of the ashram for three months. I'd like to see the whole world live in this way – no competition, no money! Once in the journal 'Osho Times,' I found an article about enlightened masters of our time. Osho is generally very critical of all types of gurus. He nevertheless acknowledged Meher Baba as enlightened. I had not heard His name before. I read that He really was an enlightened Master; that He worked with masts, *fakirs* and lepers. He created special ashrams for them all over India. I realised that Meher Baba was with those unfortunates who were not allowed in the ashram of Osho. In fact, Meher Baba went out of His way searching for these people and helped them. I became very interested and thought it would be good to find Meher Baba's grave; to bow, to touch with gratitude and connect with an enlightened Being. I began asking local *sanyasis* about Him, but very few had heard of Him. One of them told me how to get to the Samadhi, the sacred tomb of Meher Baba, which is located about 100 km from Pune.

At the Samadhi of Osho, where his ashes are kept, an evening meditation is conducted in the dark. And several times I resonated with this space and had a mental connect with him. The last time there was this connection, he told me: 'Now your *hara* is clean and you can go.' I found that I did not wish to go anywhere. But somehow a few days later, on my birthday, we were given the day off and both Elana and I went to Meherabad.

We were on the path that leads to Meher Baba's Samadhi – a quiet, deserted place. It was very hot and there were no other visitors around. A Samadhi attendant greeted us with the words, 'Jai Baba!' Inside, we saw a huge portrait of Baba which in the first instant I did not even realise was a portrait – I thought it was a real person sitting there. Then looking at it deeply, it dawned on me that this is the 'sparrow-man' whom I saw long ago in a vision: a man with a big, long nose like a beak, black eyes, and long, curly hair. If you look at the portrait from a certain angle, it looks very much like that of a bird. At least, that's how I visualised His image for the first time. I felt that it was He, the Master, the Voice, which is in contact with me! My spiritual search and all my visions came together at this one point.

I sat on a mat inside the Samadhi, closed my eyes and began

to go deep within. With the tips of the fingers of my right hand, I began to penetrate into some kind of energy, warmth and bliss. It rose above to the heart and began to flow there. This energy I recognised as love; but love not human, which is limited, but Love Divine, the infinite, boundless ocean of love. And, I knew that this is something that is worth living for. My mind darted here and there to understand what had happened. I even opened my eyes and started looking around but nothing was there – just a large marble slab, where it says 'Eternal Beloved Avatar Meher Baba'. I do not know how much time I spent there.

I knew that I would definitely be back in Meherabad because this was the place I had been searching for all my life! And Meher Baba was exactly that Being who has assisted me in the most climactic moments of my life. I recognised and felt His energy; knew His name; recognised His face! Besides, the journey to the Samadhi seemed familiar to me – the railway, the hill, the pillar of light in which I was enveloped – I had seen it all before in my visions.

In early 2004, I came back to Meherabad. Now, everything was different here. The first person with whom I became closely acquainted and felt a connection was Erico Nadel. It was now that I first saw a video of the living form of Baba. It made a deep impression on me. His every movement, every gesture was remarkable, and I was deeply imbued with love and trust in Him. I felt, and knew in my heart, that Meherabad was a fertile ground for self-knowledge and spiritual growth.

Erico once offered me night-watch duty on the Samadhi hill. It was a great opportunity for me to stay 'alone' with Baba so I gladly accepted. That evening on the way to the Samadhi, Erico told me a story.

When Erico arrived in Meherabad, Mehera, the closest disciple of Baba, was still alive; Mehera was His beloved, the feminine aspect of God in human form. She told him that when she will go to Baba, at that time Russians will come in Meherabad. 'One of them is our man. Please take care of him and do everything for him, that you can,' she had told him. Before leaving the world, Baba had told her that this Russian was charged with a mission and would lead many of his countrymen to Meherabad. Erico admitted that he felt this Russian, whom Mehera was talking about, was I. It seemed so incredible to me. During that night shift,

Meher Baba

I really felt that in each one of us is the seed of Divine Truth, but most of us are unaware of it, and 'waking the grain' is the role of the Master.

As I learned later, the Samadhi of the Avatar is a spiritual centre of our planet and, according to Meher Baba, people who come to the Samadhi, at whatever level of consciousness they may be, will always be in contact with Him. Baba also predicted that there would be a period of major disasters, both natural and man-made. As a result, there will be a powerful cleansing and people will be brought closer to God. This cleansing is inevitable, but the exact date was never divulged.

The very first time I came to Meherazad (Baba's Home), I felt an atmosphere of love and peace, renewing and giving a fresh breath of spiritual freedom.

In Meherazad, on this day, I knelt in front of Baba's chair in Mandali Hall. As I bent forward, I clearly saw Baba's legs and, without looking up, touched His feet with my hands and head. At that moment, I found myself in the indescribable bliss of complete surrender and dissolution in the ocean of unconditional love and acceptance.

Each time I found it increasingly difficult to leave Meherabad, and only the opportunity to share my experience with others inspired me to return to Russia. My purpose seemed crystal clear – to carry His message, bring His word primarily to the people of Russia; to those who were willing to hear.

It so happened that in 2008, I was staying in Meherabad at a time when it is closed to pilgrims for repairs. This happens every year when it's hot, but I did not leave. I took a room in a private home nearby, because I liked to plunge and merge with Baba as deeply as possible. There I met an Indian by the name of Nalin Dev, known in his time as a Bollywood playback singer. After hearing the story of what happened to my wife, he exclaimed, 'Oh, that's interesting! I know a lady, her name is Nan Umrigar who, through her son Karl in the other world, communicates with Baba and gets answers to various questions. He spoke of his friends in Bollywood who had asked for and received help. He himself had come to Meherabad, thanks to Nan and her book *Sounds of Silence*. Nalin helped arrange a meeting with her.

A week later I met Nan in Pune. I had prepared a few questions about my missing wife, about my past life, and also my current mission. A few days later I received a reply from her, which just struck me as so true. Karl confirmed that in a past life and in previous incarnations too, I had been with the Avatar and that Baba was very happy to meet again with me. About the events connected with my wife – it wasn't yet time to open this information because it raises an issue about the life and fate of other people too.

During these days, I had other very deep contacts with Baba and I wish to share them with you.

In a vision, I find myself sitting one day on a bench beside the road in a state of some frustration and anguish. I want privacy and I'm trying hard to get rid of some cheerful companions who are persistently inviting me somewhere and blocking my way with mocking remarks. Suddenly Baba appeared near me and took my hand in His. 'Don't worry, be happy!' was said in silence. Just then, I heard a beautiful voice and turned around. Seated on the bench was a young and very handsome man, who looked like some mystical Indian prince. He spoke in an unknown language but I understood it. It flowed like the most beautiful song from his lips.

The frivolous and mocking people suddenly froze and began to listen to him with tears in their eyes. I looked into the eyes of this young man, and felt the wonderful experience of the inner unity of our hearts. I remembered his few last words, '... Baba will show you the way.' I decided to request Nan to ask Karl if I had really met with Him? Nan promised to ask, as she too was interested. I had just finished reading her book, when I received a response from her, in which Karl spoke in plain text.

'Dear Mikhail,

You have a hotline to Baba. He can reach you whenever it is necessary for Him to do so. He can make you travel at will, go places and, at the same time, remain in close contact with Him.

Yes, I did look deeply into your heart and you did see the look in my eyes, which revealed to you that you have a special reason to be in Meherabad at this time. This will be revealed to you by Baba in due course.

Love, Karl.'

After this, I was determined that *Sounds of Silence,* which was a living soul's journey from ignorance to spiritual heights, should be translated as I wanted people to read it in Russia. Along with my new friend Jehangir Jeejeebhoy of Mumbai, with whom we met through an intuitive hint from Nan, we sorted out the formalities and signed a licensing agreement with the publisher that this book could be published in Russia. It took a year, and on August 30, 2011, *Sounds of Silence – a bridge across two worlds* was published in Russian on Russian soil.

When I think back on the time when I had not heard of Meher Baba; when I did not even know His name, or the fact that He existed, I realise how much I have changed. No matter how strong the power of the illusion of separateness may be, no matter how strong our attachment to the material world; it is nothing when compared to the infinite ocean of love one receives from the Master. My life no longer has worldly goals. I try to serve Meher Baba by helping seekers to find the path; to turn within and realise one's own higher Self.

Avatar Meher Baba Ki Jai!

The Russian edition of *Sounds of Silence* has been published by Aikya Publishing, Kirov.

CHAPTER 13

From Art to Heart

So, you have just been around the world with Baba. Read on and see where He is going to be taking you now ...

Baba loved going to the movies. There is great power in the spoken word and when coupled with music and dancing, it becomes even more potent. But Baba's purpose in going to the movies was more to establish His internal contact with spectators for their spiritual benefit.

The Mandali who accompanied Baba on these occasions would state that Baba would remain in the theatre only for a short time, and then leave the theatre in the middle of the screening when He knew His work was completed. Baba had stated, *'The film world has magnificent scope to tell the world about spiritual things they should know. Those who see films forget themselves and put their hearts and minds into the show. They forget their worries and the world. The most important thing for one is to forget oneself to realize God.'*[1]

When travelling abroad, Baba would go to the movies in Madrid, Zurich, Port Said, London, New York, Paris and Cannes. He visited Hollywood to forge a link with the film world and met with several actors and directors. He saw many films, and He was also filmed in return.

The medium of the screen thus served another purpose. It helped show the Avatar in action, dictating on His alphabet board. Baba said that in time to come, people would get illumination through seeing Him on the screen for, *'there is no more powerful instrument for stimulating the imagination than the moving pictures. It inspires those who see them to a greater understanding, truer feeling, better lives and need not have anything to do with religion – real spirituality is best portrayed in stories of pure love, selfless service, of truth realised and applied to the most humble circumstances of our daily lives.'*[2]

Mahiema Anand

Way back in 2002, I stumbled upon a title for a project I was considering to do. It was called 'Sounds of Silence'. Little did I know that this thought alone would become the starting point of a long and endless journey.

One day, I happened to mention this title to a friend of mine who promptly took out a book with the same title and asked me to read it. Never having heard about the book or the author before, I took it up casually and started to read. Then, totally caught up by its first few pages, I finished reading it in just one night. Next morning, the first thing on my agenda was to locate the author, Nan Umrigar. I tried calling everyone I could for leads on her, but my efforts were unsuccessful. And then I just forgot all about it.

Another project of mine took me to Athens where I had to make a presentation. Though it went well, a comment by someone from the audience shook me up a bit. Feeling upset and brooding over that at lunch, I was surprised when a lady from London asked if she could join me. Seeing the frame of mind I was in, she took out a card from her bag and extended it toward me. It had a picture of Meher Baba with the saying, **'Don't Worry Be Happy!'**

I don't know why but the first question I asked her was: 'Do you happen to know Nan Umrigar?' She said she knew someone in London who did and that she would try to get the details for me. True to her word, as soon as I landed back in India, I got a mail from Anita Ramchandani from London with Nan's contact details in Pune. I could not wait another moment and called her on the phone. But I was in for a surprise – she happened to be in Mumbai that very day! We met for lunch at McDonalds and I just sat there listening wide-eyed to all her wonderful stories about Karl and his appearances.

My belief in 'the other side' has always been unshakeable and I've always felt that both the worlds co-exist. I had always wanted to present all this as a documentary for television. The way it was usually portrayed in cinema or on television used to upset me a lot and, somewhere, as a film maker, I wanted to make a difference. My mind started ticking. Perhaps Karl was one way of getting there? At the time, I was doing a show on the paranormal for Zee TV, so I suggested Karl and Nan's story to the channel, but my idea was turned down. Yet, I did not give up hope.

The next year, Reality TV from London gave us a contract to create ten stories of human interest pertaining to India. So I quietly squeezed in Nan's story in the lot of ten which of course got approved. But there was one condition: the channel did not want a story with any religious or spiritual connotation, so I was asked not to put any information regarding Meher Baba in the film. It was a disturbing clause but I accepted it, as a beginning to something unknown. So, we shot for a day at Nan's house in Pune. I will always remember the experience as something fulfilling – no pressure of work, and the whole atmosphere was charged with an air of peace that cannot be explained in words. The entire lot of ten films was sent to London after the edit. This particular story was received the best – not only by the channel people, but also by their viewers.

Meanwhile, Anita was coming down to Mumbai and we were to meet up for the very first time. She called to say that she had booked me along with her to go to Meherabad. I did not know what to expect from this, as other than what I had read in Nan's book, I hardly knew anything about Meher Baba. Anyway, I went along. I was taken to the Samadhi and I sat there not knowing what to do or say. So I just looked up at His picture and said to Him, 'I don't know why You've got me here, Baba? I don't even know much about You, so if You want me to go back with some kind of belief, please appear before me in flesh and blood before I leave.' And I left it at that. The next morning, everyone from the Pilgrim Centre was taken to Baba's home at Meherazad and there, to my disbelief, I actually saw Him! We were collected in the dark room and shown a complete blown-up screen preview of Baba's film! I actually saw Him, large as life. I came back to Mumbai, a little shocked, but also happy!

After that, very conveniently, Baba took a back seat in my life for almost two years. Although the very next year He showed me a glimpse of Himself once more, the fool that I was, I did not see it. I still refused to see the larger picture! I was working on a project of global peace for children of the world, and had been invited by Deepak Chopra to Puerto Rico for a conference called 'Alliance for New Humanity'. I was to make a presentation along with Ricky Martin and Betty Williams. This was a God-sent opportunity and I kept asking myself what had I done to deserve this? The gentleman I was coordinating with was a very sweet man called Arsenio Rodrigues from Puerto Rico. Once, I dialled his cell and was routed to his voice mail asking me to leave a message and, at the end of his recorded message, he said, 'Jai Baba'. It gave me such a jolt and set me thinking – which Baba was this?

This question remained in my mind from the time I landed in Puerto Rico and throughout the three-day conference. When I was to leave, Arsenio gave me a hug and asked which part of Mumbai I lived in. I asked him if he had ever visited India, to which he answered that he often goes to a place called Meherabad to visit the Meher Baba Samadhi. Aha! I had got my answer to the 'Baba' on voicemail! He then told me his story. Apparently, the 'Alliance for New Humanity' was the brainchild of Meher Baba. Arsenio had prayed to Him, and then left the whole thing to Baba. To organise an international conference in a place like Puerto Rico was no mean task. And yet Baba had made all this happen! I was more than just impressed.

In August, a friend of mine who was living in the US approached me about a spiritual film festival to be held in California. As most of the subjects for my films have been spiritual in nature, she felt I might have a film I could submit. Since I had none ready at that time, she asked me to create one. I gave this some serious thought for a few days, until a possibility emerged. As I had shot enough material about Karl and Nan for my previous film, all I needed was to shoot some more and, maybe add Baba to the film this time. Yes, I thought, that would make it a complete feature! I picked up the phone, called Nan and discussed my idea with her. She was very positive but said that I would have to go through protocol and get all the necessary permissions to shoot in and around locations at Meherabad. So, I immediately sent out emails to acquire the permissions. In less than a week, I had all the permissions sitting in my inbox.

I had planned a film with a running time of ten minutes that would require just one or two days of shooting, so I decided to put in funds from my own pocket. But then I received a mail from my friend in America specifying that the minimum duration of the film had to be twenty minutes. So now what? I did not have the money to make a longer film. Anyhow, I just went ahead. I started working on the story. Since I knew very little about Baba or Meherabad, I had to connect with someone who could provide me with all the information that I needed. The following week, a business dinner at a friend's place turned out to be the beginning of a series of miracles that were to continue in the months to come. In spiritual terms, we call this synchronicity. I was introduced to a lady called Indrani Rathore who worked with another TV channel. We had the most innocuous and irrelevant conversation all evening until, at parting time, she offered to give me a lift in her car. As soon as I got in, I saw three pictures of Meher Baba stuck all over the dashboard of her car. Before closing the door, I looked at her and asked the obvious question. She said she was married into a Baba lover's family. Then, of course, she wanted to know what I had to do with Him. When I mentioned that I was keen on making a film on Him, she got even more excited, and our evening extended till 4 am! The icing on the cake was when we both entered the same complex and found that we lived just a block away from each other!

I entered her house and came face to face with a huge portrait of Baba. Whichever direction of the room I went to, His eyes followed me. It felt as though I was constantly being watched over by Him. Well, Indrani told me about her life and her leanings towards Baba. Then somewhere in the middle of our conversation, she got up to get me something and returned with about half-a-dozen books on Baba, written by her father-in-law, Prof. Rathore, who lives near the Samadhi at Meherabad. So here was my answer to all the academic information I needed on Baba!

Before I left her house at four in the morning, Indrani asked me if I still had any doubts about the making of the film. Of course I did. Where was the money to come from? She asked me to drop that doubt right there at His feet and ask Him to take care of it. Well, having no choice in the matter, I decided to do just that and went back to my place and slept. I was woken up at 10 am by Nan's call. She gave me a couple of telephone numbers of some people who had approached her for making a film on Baba. She thought maybe they could share their ideas with me, as we all seemed to be planning the very same thing. I called up the gentleman, Suresh Dagur in Pune. He said he was flying off to Hong Kong that very night but was willing to spend a few minutes over coffee with me in Mumbai, before leaving for the airport. We met very briefly that same evening and before I knew it, I had a producer for the film!

All these experiences should have taught me that I'm not the 'doer' but, the ego being strong, I did not want to lose control over the project. How can I explain to you that every event that occurred from then on toward the making of the film was nothing short of a miracle? So much so that, by the end of it, I felt that I had had conversations with God at every step of the way. Never in my life had I felt that way before!

Now that the money was also in place, work on the film began. While the script was being written, many encouraging messages were coming our way from Karl and the 'other side'. They were beautiful leads for us to follow yet, at the same time, were scary as the responsibility on our shoulders was immense. Time and again, one particular message kept coming from Baba that this film should focus entirely on 'love'. This became the biggest challenge ever for me. How was I to portray this expression vividly on screen?

I decided to start off with the love of a mother for her child – to portray as well as I could the journey of a mother to reach God through her son who had passed on. Yes, her journey was through a tool called auto writing, but it was all inspired by love. To many Baba lovers, this was a practice of the *occult*. So there were very good chances of us getting flak from some people, and also being responsible for hurting the sentiments of others. We were walking a tight rope! But I think Baba also had His plans for me. I was guided so beautifully at every step, and most of all by my producer Sureshji. He was a tough taskmaster and a very difficult man to please. But his constant nagging for perfection, and his insistence to include as much of Baba as possible, made me strive harder. He was determined to get it just right. It took us nearly six months to complete the film, but for me it was worth it all because that is what brought me closer to Baba. This is the essence of life.

Troubles and pain are part of our growth. However, as we develop faith and surrender to a higher power, we can walk the path in peace and joy.

The film is now completed. When we look at it, we wonder if we actually made it! It's not our work, it's the work of God!

And, ever since, I have never forgotten Baba.

———————

Baba said, *'Art when inspired with Love leads to higher realms. Love art, and that art will open for you the inner life. When you are lost in it, your ego diminishes, Love infinite appears, and when Love is created, God is attained. So you see how art can lead one to Infinite God.'*

— *Baba and the Theatre* by Delia de Leon

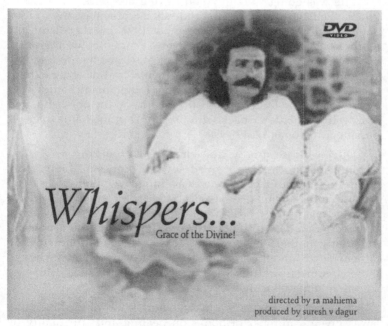

The cover of the DVD 'Whispers...' filmed by Mahiema.
This DVD is available from Cyrus Khambata, Mobile: 9821009715 or Nan Umrigar, Mobile: 9822391533.

Let us see what Neha Sharad has to tell us about her love of art and how it led her to Baba.

Neha Sharad

I am the youngest of three daughters of parents who were renowned artists. My father was the writer Padmashri Sharad Joshi, and my mother, Irfana Sharad, was a stage actress. It was a union of love and they took a conscious decision not to allow religion to create any kind of complications in their or their children's lives. I was therefore born in a family where God or religion did not play a prominent role. I had a carefree childhood, surrounded by an atmosphere of literature and the arts.

Life was going smoothly and during this period my sisters got married. However, my first rude shock came with the sudden demise of my father on 5th September 1991. Six days later, my mother had a stroke. For the next few years our life became a nightmare. My mother suffered the most, as she had to undergo several surgeries. Added to it was the mental trauma of my father's loss. During these nine years my mother fought many battles – her desire to join my father in the other world on the one hand, and our desire to hold her back with us. She won the battle over us; passing away on 6th July 1999.

During those nine years when I was working as well as nursing my mother, I received several hints and clues from different sources. Once there was a strange telephone call saying that my father wanted to speak to me. Someone even sent me the book *Laws of the Spirit World* by the Bhavnagris. I was led to an expert on auto writing but my upbringing, my frame of mind due to my mother's health, the chaos in the family following my father's death, and the sudden responsibility thrust on me due to these circumstances prevented me from going deeper, or paying attention to these incidents.

After 1996, I was drawn to Reiki and other forms of healing. I was given a number of books on healing and spirituality by people I did not even know. This reading made me aware of these healing arts. The first step of recognition of this growing faith took me to a temple of Shirdi Sai Baba.

October 2002 marks my introduction and the beginnings of a relationship with Meher Baba. The entire month saw me receiving books and seeing pictures of Meher Baba. I heard a great deal about Baba from different sources. It all culminated with my receiving a copy of Nan Umrigar's *Sounds of Silence.* I read the book and it brought home all the experiences of my parent's efforts to communicate with me. Three days after completing the book, I found myself on the road to Meherabad. I was sure I was going to the right place and on the way I prayed to Baba to give me a signal that my parents were with Him.

I had my first darshan at the Samadhi of Baba and went to sit in front of His tomb. Within a few minutes, a lady came to me and asked, 'Are you Sharad Joshi's daughter? Where is Irfana?' This came as a shock to me but, in an instant, I understood what Baba was conveying to me. I was thrilled.

In December 2002, on my second visit to Meherabad, I chanced upon Rupam who was also helped by Nan Umrigar and has become an absolute believer in Meher Baba. She very kindly offered to introduce me to Nan, who was her close friend. My first meeting with Nan took place on 14th December 2002 in Pune and it resulted in a firmer faith of my parent's existence on another plane. Karl informed me that my parents are together, that they are with Baba, and that they have decided to lead their further life together! They conveyed to me that they were also very pleased that I had finally made contact with them. I was now at peace.

Since then, a few years have passed. I have progressed spiritually and do not need these kind of assurances anymore. I am now into healing through Baba and He is guiding me at every step. He has enabled me to meet many eminent healers. I also have several patients coming to me for healing. I attribute it to Baba's Grace that He is providing me with this direction. One recent incident that comes to mind is that of a four-day old blue baby from Bangalore. Her parents were frantically asking for help because the baby had to be operated within two days and there were three operations that would be performed on this baby. One surgery was for the heart and the others for the lungs. My Reiki energy was amplified by Baba's energy as I had appealed to Baba for this healing on the baby, for the doctor, and for the hospital she was admitted in. I had spent the previous night in channelling Baba's energy to them. On the day of the surgery,

I saw Baba, in the course of my meditation, standing near the baby and operating on her! Around 10.30 am when the actual surgery started, the doctors found the baby so healthy that they decided to do all three operations at one go instead of doing them on three separate days.

I was at Baba's Samadhi on my birthday that was on 28th February 2003. It was a wonderfully moving experience to see all the *Sufis* there with their guitars and singing at the Samadhi. They wished me for my birthday and I felt I had been enveloped by the love of my parents, and my Baba. I returned home from this visit feeling energised and overflowing with Baba's Love.

After my return, and during my meditation, I asked Karl to give me a sign if he had been around me, and a strange thing happened. For the past few days, a friend of mine had been insisting that I treat her to the film 'Catch Me If You Can,' in celebration of my birthday. I had no cash on me, as I had not been able to go to the bank. I asked Baba for help and guess what! In the afternoon, I had an unexpected visit from a family friend who gifted me Rs.1000 as a belated birthday gift! I smiled, said thanks to Baba, and went with my friend for the movie.

Did I see Karl? The answer is yes. He was there in the shape of the hero Karl played by Tom Hanks! Maybe it was my imagination but I found the incident more than significant, for in the film, Karl once again helps to bring back to his roots, a boy lost along the way.

By now my father's fame had spread far and wide and I was invited to read his poems and articles in the West Indies, Canada and the UK. All the documents and other preparations were complete, except for one critical document i.e. the US transit visa. I suddenly realised on the day of my flight that I needed an immigration clearance for the Port of Spain. The consulates of both these countries are in the south end of the city and I reside in the north end.

I rushed to the US embassy only to discover that I was late and it had closed. What could I do? I did nothing but pray to Baba to help me with these formalities. And Baba on His part was actively getting these formalities completed for me. You might wonder how? The organisers of my trip were able to impress upon the US consulate the urgency of my transit visa. Quite possibly, this may have been one of the very rare instances when the doors were reopened and my passport duly stamped. I received my immigration letter for Port of Spain at the Mumbai airport. It took me considerable time and effort to believe that I was in an aircraft flying on schedule to the West Indies.

If this was not enough, I had further exhilarating evidence of Baba's Grace, during my six-week tour! I was fortunate to have the darshan of my *Sadguru* Shri Sai Baba of Shirdi, who was instrumental in leading me to Meher Baba. This came on every Thursday in the form of pictures and a temple in every country that I visited during my journey. If this is also not a marvel of Baba's Grace, what is?

Before I conclude, I would like to share a beautiful incident with readers. One day I was sitting in the Rahuri Cabin at Lower Meherabad, in front of Baba's picture. A young girl was sitting beside me, just in front of my friend, Dr. Vasudha Kothari. As I finished my prayers and stood up, I just bent and kissed the girl's forehead and came out. Vasudha asked me if I knew the girl and we both chuckled when I said I had never seen her before. Next morning during breakfast, the girl came up to meet us and introduced herself as Meher Meenbattiwala. She mentioned that on her birthday, the day earlier, while she was sitting in the Rahuri Cabin, she was asking Baba to show her a sign of His love. 'At that very moment, you came and gave me a kiss on my forehead!' she said. I smiled and that smile is growing each day because I am under the wings of Meher Baba. Thanks Baba!

CHAPTER 14

Baba's Silence

'Throughout eternity I have laid down principles and precepts, but mankind has ignored them. Man's inability to live God's words makes the Avatar's teaching a mockery. Instead of practicing the compassion He taught, man has waged crusades in His name. Instead of living the humility, purity and truth of His words, man has given way to hatred, greed and violence.

Because man has been deaf to the principles and precepts laid down by God in the past, in this present avataric form I observe Silence.'[1]

A group of youngsters from Pune were all excited and lined up to go to Meherabad. For me too it was almost like a new experience for I had not been able to do this for three years since the day I broke my hip. However, I was better now and so, after the bus dropped us at Meherabad, I took them on a visit to the Samadhi to pay homage to Beloved Baba. Then I decided to start our tour at the old Pilgrim Centre and we made our way towards it.

Going back to that old building revived memories of the first time I had gone to Meherabad in 1985: how I had met so many of the old Baba lovers – Dolly and Jal Dastur, Heather Nadel, Alan Wagner and Gary Kleiner, and unbelievable as it may seem, they were all still there twenty-seven years later. They greeted me warmly and hugged me – it felt like I was coming home again.

I walked through the garden with the group still thinking about old times – walked under the same old trees, past the graves of the men Mandali, past the basketball court, past the Table House where Baba wrote His book, past Mohammed the Mast's quarters, and into the old Mandali Hall where we saw old pictures of the

130

Perfect Masters, the chart of the evolution of consciousness, and took darshan of Baba's Chair.

As soon as we walked out of there we came back to Baba's *Jhopdi* – the place where Baba started His Silence and never spoke again for the rest of the fourty-four years of His life.

The group of youngsters listened carefully to all that I had to say but it was what they saw and heard about Baba's Silence that had all the newcomers totally fascinated. They were so eager with their questions:

Q. Forty-four years! Baba kept complete Silence for forty-four years? That's so hard to believe! You mean this is the very place that Baba entered and never spoke another word after that? How did it all begin?

A. Well ... before Baba began His continuous and unbroken Silence on 10th July 1925, He had kept Silence intermittently on a few occasions for short durations. But in June 1925, Baba made a declaration to the Mandali – His close disciples staying with Him – that He will have to keep Silence for a longer duration of about a year or a year-and-a-half, and that it would commence from the 10th of July. He clarified that this is not to be taken as a penance of some sort or a spiritual exercise on His part, as He had nothing more to achieve or gain. His Silence concerned the future of the world and was kept solely for the benefit of humanity.

Meher Baba's Jhopdi.

When a local schoolteacher from the Hazrat Babajan School pleaded with Baba that if He became silent, how would He teach, Baba replied, *'I have come not to teach, but to Awaken!'*[2] These were to be His last words to anyone outside of His circle, and this message was the meaning of His Divine mission to the world.

And yes, speaking of Hazrat Babajan, one of the five Perfect Masters, Baba had also indicated that one reason for Him to observe a prolonged silence concerned Hazrat Babajan: *'I must keep silence for some excessive spiritual work that will result when Babajan drops her body in the near future.'*[3]

Q. Did He leave any last moment instructions for His followers living with Him?

A. Yes, indeed! He was the most practical and meticulous Master. On the 8th of July 1925, two days before He commenced His Silence, He called a meeting of the men Mandali and instructed each person about their specific duties during the coming year-or-so of Silence. He exhorted the Mandali to use their bodies for the service of others and asked them to take care of their health.

Q. But, what actually happened on the 10th of July? He just stopped speaking?

A. Well, first let me tell you what happened a day before. On the 9th of July 1925, Baba once again explained everything to everyone in great detail. All duties and responsibilities of everyone were clearly spelt out. Only five men were nominated to speak with Baba, and that too concerning their assigned duties and only at a specified time each day.

Likewise, Baba visited the women's quarters and gave instructions about their duties. He asked them to take good care of their health and cook food for all the school children as if they were cooking for their own children.

Then at around eight in the evening, Baba visited the men Mandali's quarters and once again told them that He would be silent from the next day; that they should take care of everything at Meherabad as they had been doing all along. He asked them not to worry about anything and that everything in Meherabad will run smoothly if they discharged their duties properly and obeyed His instructions. He again emphasised that they should take care of their health.

And yes, another important instruction that Baba gave before retiring to His Jhopdi was, *'Whenever you go out during the night, always carry a lantern. Beware of snakes! I will save you from every calamity under the sun, but I won't help you if you are bitten by a snake. So be careful.'*[4]

It was 8.30 pm when He concluded His instructions and then said: *'I am going to the Jhopdi now. All of you go to bed.'*[5]

Q. *And then from the next day, He was silent?*

A. Wait, wait, don't be in such a hurry, the day has not yet ended. Then something dramatic happened. Padri, one of the Mandali, went out to answer nature's call and he had barely gone a few steps when he spotted a cobra in his path. During those days, the place was infested with snakes and scorpions but not anymore, so don't you worry. So Padri shouted, 'Snake! Snake!' The other men came running out with their staves and Baba came out of His Jhopdi to inquire what the commotion was all about. When Baba was informed about the snake, He was pleased that Padri had obeyed His instructions of carrying a lantern.

He then walked over to the women's quarters and spoke with them briefly, telling them how fortunate they were in hearing His voice so many times in the day, and also that the incident about the snake offered them another opportunity to hear Him speak for the final time.

Q. *And then from next day. Baba stopped speaking?*

A. Yes. He got up at five the next morning – Friday, 10th July 1925 – and went about inquiring as usual about the Mandali's work, school children's health, sleep and food, and performed all the activities as usual, but with a difference – instead of speaking, He wrote out notes. And in this manner the days rolled into weeks, and then months and years. But though He was silent, those around Him felt Baba becoming more and more dynamic in His daily activities.

Baba had such a beautiful voice and His nature was so outgoing that He often broke out spontaneously into song or poetry. Many in the Mandali doubted if He would be able to keep silence for that long a time. But as days passed, they were highly impressed to observe that the Master never spoke even once. He was always in perfect control of Himself. Baba loved music so much that He would still participate in the bhajan programmes, His hands would be heard playing a drum; or beating time with the singers in harmony. But His beautiful voice was never heard again.

Q. So instead of speaking, He conducted all His activities throughout His lifetime by writing?

A. No. Initially He wrote, either on paper with pencil or pen, or on slates with chalk. The bunch of slates was quite cumbersome as they were required to be carried wherever He went. However, after completing His yet unpublished Book, about which I'll talk later, He stopped writing altogether from January 1927.

Q. Did He actually write a Book?

A. Yes. Three days after He stopped speaking, He started writing a mysterious Book from the 13th of July 1925. This work too commenced in His Jhopdi. Every day, after His early morning bath, He would start writing from 5 am till about 8.30 am. After that, He would be busy with His other duties. Baba indicated having used several languages in writing the Book and revealed that it contains hitherto unknown spiritual secrets. The Book in its entirety has not been read by anyone. You see this Table House? This was where much of the Book was also written. It was specially built in October of the same year, but its original location was elsewhere – more towards the main road. It was the most precious Book and Baba carried it everywhere He went – including the time He went abroad to the West. The Book was encased in a metal box casing that had a locking device.

From time to time, the Book was also kept in safe custody of various Banks in India and abroad.

Q. Sorry to interrupt, Nan, but where is it now?

A. Wish I knew that! A few days before Baba dropped His physical Form, one of the Mandali, I think it was Eruch, asked Baba about the whereabouts of the Book and Baba gestured indicating that it is safe and will come out when the time is right. Hence, no one knows its whereabouts. We can safely conclude that Baba knows His business and when the time is right, it would be revealed to humanity.

Q. You said that thereafter He completely stopped writing? How did He manage to communicate?

A. He did not stop writing altogether. He would put His signature or initials wherever absolutely necessary, such as on important documents, or wherever it pleased Him!

So far as His communication is concerned, initially He would point at the letters or words in the newspaper to convey His thoughts. But this was a slow and cumbersome process. And so Chanji, one of His Mandali, typed the English alphabets in capital letters on a piece of paper which Baba began carrying with Him to spell out words. Still later, the alphabets and the numerals from 0 to 9 were painted on a handy ply board and it came to be known as His alphabet board, which He started using from the 7th of January 1927 and continued using for many years.

Q. Many years? Not all through His life?

A. That's right. He discarded the use of the alphabet board from 7th October 1954 and thereafter only relied on His unique hand and facial gestures to communicate. The Mandali were quite adept at reading both the board, as well as His gestures.

Q. Wow! How interesting!

A. And intriguing too.

Q. But Baba was to keep His Silence only for a year or so. Why did He not break it?

A. Frankly, Baba's business, Baba alone knows. But it is a fact that at times He indicated that He would be breaking His Silence on a particular day, but that date would pass by without Baba apparently breaking His Silence. This happened quite a few times. No one can authentically say, even those amongst His Mandali, whether Baba has broken or is yet to break His Silence. It is indeed quite intriguing.

Even His messages concerning the breaking of His silence are not easy to comprehend and sometimes seem to be contradictory. Perhaps that is the reason why Baba often cautioned us all, **'Do not try to understand Me. My depth is unfathomable. Just love Me.'**[6] And the best part is that those who are most concerned with Beloved Baba, are least concerned about whether or not He had broken His Silence. They just love Him, anyway.

Q. What is your personal take, Nan, on this? Do you think He has broken His Silence?

A. Well, frankly, of the numerous messages that Beloved Baba had given out concerning His Silence and the breaking of His Silence, the one that touches my heart most is this one: *'When the Word of My Love, breaks out of its Silence and speaks in your hearts, telling you who I really am, you will know that that is the Real word you have always been longing to hear.'*[7] As a prelude to this message, Baba indicated, *'You have had enough words; I have had enough words. It is not through words that I give what I have to give. In the silence of your perfect surrender, My Love which is always Silent can flow to you – to be yours always to keep and to share with those who seek Me.'*[8] Aren't they beautiful and profound words coming from the God-Man Himself?

Coming to your question; yes, Baba has broken His silence in my heart and that is why I am here. You all know from my first book *Sounds of Silence* that I was not at all the religious type. And what a way Beloved Baba entered my life and how He orchestrated everything thereafter to help me share His beauty and His bountiful Love all around! Words are just not enough to express my feelings. I am eternally thankful to Him.

––––––––––

The Question-Answer session was over but, fired by this renewed enthusiasm, I felt the urge to rediscover from Baba literature what else He had to say on this very absorbing and fascinating subject. And this is what I found:

When asked why He observed silence, Baba replied:

'If you were to ask Me why I do not talk, I would say, mostly for three reasons. Firstly, I feel that through you all I am talking eternally. Secondly, to relieve the boredom of talking incessantly through your forms, I keep silence in My personal physical form. And thirdly, because all talk in itself is idle talk. Lectures, messages, statements, discourses of any kind spiritual or otherwise, imparted through utterances or writings, is just idle talk when not acted upon or lived up to.'[9]

Another beautiful one: *'Man's inability to live God's words makes the Avatar's teaching a mockery. Instead of practicing the compassion He taught, man has waged crusades in His name.*

Instead of living the humility, purity, and truth of His words, man has given way to hatred, greed, and violence. Because man has been deaf to the principles and precepts laid down by God in the past, in this present Avataric form, I observe silence.'[10]

And then the most beautiful of all: *'I am never silent. I speak eternally. The voice that is heard deep within the Soul is My voice – the voice of inspiration, of intuition, of guidance. To those who are receptive to this voice, I speak.''*[11]

It may not be out of place to mention that a few of Beloved Baba's statements issued during His ministry on earth were cryptic and carried with them their mystical ambiguity. They were not meant to contradict reason or confuse anyone; they only illustrated the inability of words to explain or express the deeper mystical aspects of Baba's inner spiritual working.

For many years, Baba had asked His followers to observe silence or to fast on 10th July. However, in His Life Circular issued in May 1968, which was the last issued on the subject of silence, He had asked His lovers and those who would like to do so, to observe complete silence for twenty-four hours from the midnight of 9th July till the midnight of 10th July (local time, I suppose). The option for fasting was not given.

While Meher Baba did not establish any special on-going requirement of His followers to keep silence, the majority of His lovers love to observe silence on the 10th of July every year, on an informal and voluntary basis, in honour of His last wish.

It is quite an experience indeed!

The many moods of Baba's 'Silence'.

CHAPTER 15

The Mighty Heart

It was 7th October 2006 when I first got a call from Charu Malik who was in Delhi at the time. Her young son Alok had just passed away and someone had told her about my book *Sounds of Silence*. Reading about Karl Umrigar reminded her of school days when she was in the same class as him.

Charu was keen to contact her son as she felt there were some unspoken thoughts and words that had been left unexchanged and unsaid between them. Just before he went into the ICU, he had desperately wanted to tell her something but the doctors could not allow him to do so.

The very first message she got from Alok put her mind at rest. He managed to tell her all he had wanted to say and Charu began to breathe freely again. I say breathe because, as I got to know her better, I got the distinct impression that here was one mighty heart that was not going to allow adverse circumstances in life get the better of her.

Some months later, I happened to be in Delhi for a talk on *Sounds of Silence* in a place called Moon Beam and took the opportunity to visit Charu. Although I was aware that she was a victim of muscular dystrophy, I was certainly not prepared for what I saw. As I opened the door, I saw a well-dressed lady lying on the bed. Her hair was combed neatly back from her face and her legs were covered by a clean white blanket with a print of roses on it. Her dainty hands were covered with sparkling red bangles, and her fingers with their perfectly manicured pink nails, were crossed sedately over her chest. There was a beautiful welcoming smile on her face. As I was given a chair to sit down next to her, I noticed that her maid had to literally turn her head so that her

139

large, luminous eyes could focus on me. Two pictures hung on the wall behind her and I knew instantly that this young teenage boy was indeed her dearly beloved son Alok.

During our conversation that day she told me her heartrending story.

Charu Malik

'I love God, I love Meher Baba and, Papa, I love you very much.'

Those were the last words spoken by Alok before he left us on the 1st of December 2005. It was one of the biggest blows God could have dealt to any mother. On that day, I lost my only child. For a major part of my life, I have lived with muscular dystrophy – a slow and relentless degeneration of the muscles. One cannot do much about it and towards its later stages one is confined to a life between the bed and a wheelchair.

I was a normal child who had a lot of rosy dreams and aspirations. At the age of nineteen, I got married to Sunil, the man of my dreams ... He has been my protective angel and pillar of strength and quite literally pulled me through the trials and tribulations of the past thirty-one years of our life. The shock of hearing about my physical disorder, and our son fighting a losing battle for his life, devastated him – yet he willingly sacrificed every moment of his life for both of us.

I have always been a bit scared of hospitals, doctors and injections. So, it was rather unpleasant when at the age of twenty-one, I realised that I would have to spend a large part of life surrounded by them. I had been told that my lifespan was now limited to just about seven to ten years. Surprisingly, I never really worried about it, nor did I ever say, 'Why me?' I had believed firmly in Shirdi Sai Baba since I was a young child, and I knew that he would always be beside me. I was also clear that everything happens for a reason; that sometimes we are not aware of why certain events occur.

I was twenty-six years old when I became pregnant. I have always loved children and believed this to be Sai Baba's gift to me. Despite the fact that my affliction had progressed to a stage where even walking was difficult for me, and being fully aware of the fact that I may lose my own life during childbirth, I had decided to go ahead with the pregnancy.

Alok was born on the 26th of May 1988 and that was one of the happiest days of my life. Doctors called him a 'miracle child' because, with my medical history, they didn't quite believe I could give birth to a child. On 26th May 1981, I had lost my first child so it came as somewhat of a surprise that Alok was born – seven years later – on the same day!

Alok grew up as a normal child. He was always mindful of me, doing little things for me and pushing my wheelchair around. He always seemed to live life in the moment. I have often wondered if deep within he knew God's plan, for he had attained an amazing level of spirituality by the age of twelve and his faith in Satya Sai Baba was unshakeable.

The years passed as if in a dream. Alok was growing up well, doing well at school, and the joy and happiness around me allowed me to deal well with my illness. However, I was totally unprepared for what lay ahead. On 3rd May 2000, we came to know that Alok had kidney failure. No one could tell us why this had happened, but a kidney transplant was the only alternative. At this point in time, although I did question God yet my faith was strong enough to reassure me that Alok would be looked after, no matter what. My husband Sunil readily offered to donate a kidney and on 18th January 2001, both the people I loved most in the world were in the operation theatre at the same time. Following the transplant, Alok's faith in Satya Sai Baba was even greater than it had been. To see a child suffering so much and, yet, constantly reassuring me with his brave words: 'Mom, don't worry! We'll deal with situations as they arise,' made me realise again what a special soul my son was.

Throughout this harrowing ordeal, Alok remained calm and strong. Even though he knew that no one could do anything to ease his pain, not once did he despair or lose hope. It was now that I had some questions to put to God. Where was He when Alok was calling for help? How could He have turned a deaf ear to my cries? Even though at some point he must have realised the futility of medical treatment, Alok remained brave and cheerful. While his friends were enjoying their last year of school life, he spent his last days lying in a hospital bed. When he had been put on the ventilator in the ICU, Alok kept waving his hands as if he was trying to write something in the air. The doctor informed us that he was asking for paper, but the power of God had taken over and Alok could never write, nor get off the ventilator again.

On 1st December 2005, Alok passed away due to a fungal infection and probably a medical error – and my whole world crashed around me. I was over and done with God. I did not want to ever pray to Him again. Seeing my son's lifeless body and wanting to hug him for the last time, I slipped and dislocated my shoulder. After the cremation, I was taken to the hospital. Outside the operation theatre, on the stretcher, I saw this was the same hospital where I had given birth to Alok. It was God's way of saying, 'I gave him to you here, and now you have given him back to me.' At this low point in my life, Nan crossed my path. I met her in October 2006 when she was in Delhi for the launch of *Sounds of Silence.* I spent some precious moments with her and soon found myself reading her book.

On 17th October 2006, I got my first message from Alok. It began by Karl explaining why Alok left us so soon. It also explained what he wanted to tell us towards the end – thanking us for all the wonderful time he had spent with us, along with his wish to see me happy and taken care of for the rest of my life. He also expressed a desire to see his father happy.

The second message from Karl gave us some more answers as to why things were happening the way they were in our lives. It said, *'You have taken on his karma so that he can be freed from this burden he has carried for so long. You have opted to go through this pain because of your love for him that is why he has become free and left you in pain. Baba will also send you your gift of freedom after one more lifetime with your dear son for company.'* He assured us that Meher Baba was with Alok. Karl always gave some beautiful message about God, and I started to believe whatever he said. Deep down, I started to comfort myself with the thought that Alok had come for a reason, and that now he was with Baba in a better place. And so the messages continued coming, with a lot of signs and gifts coming our way, as proof that it was really Alok talking to us from the other world. But it was the message that came on his birthday that really sealed it all for me.

On 26th May 2007, I had asked Nan what it was that Alok would want me to do on his birthday. I had heard there were riots in Pune that day, so the message that was posted to me did not arrive in time. I had already planned to have a 'bhajan' in the house that day, which was to be performed by my cousin. As fate would have it, my cousin came with a gentleman and introduced him as Alok. I cannot put into words what I felt – tears rolled down my face – Alok had come to sing on Alok's birthday. Not only did he sing; he sang specially for me, not facing the temple, but looking at me.

The next day I called Nan and mentioned that I had not yet received my message from Karl. Someone up there had planned the entire event so perfectly. Later, when I received the message, its last line said it all for me: 'I am waiting to sing for you Mama on my birthday.' Need I say more? In this way, slowly but surely, my belief in Meher Baba and in all the messages I was getting was becoming stronger and stronger.

Sometimes we utter strange words without thinking. Soon after I lost Alok, someone said to me, 'It is very unfortunate that this has happened to you.' I answered spontaneously, 'Alok is studying in the University of God. We all have to take admission there, so it doesn't really matter if he took it before us.' To any normal person, this may sound as if this mother had probably lost her mind. My pain and sorrow at having lost my son still remains with me. However, I feel he is in a far better place than where I am. He is with Baba and so loved. What more can I ask for as a mother?

In March 2011, a temporary nurse dropped me in the bathroom and both my femur bones broke. In spite of all my determination, the question again came to my mind: 'Baba why are you doing this to me?' However immobile I had been earlier, I could still be taken out of the house in a wheelchair. But now I could not even turn in my bed. We didn't know if the doctor would be able to operate on me as I was also suffering from a major respiratory disorder; due to the progression of my disease, the lungs and heart had started giving away.

Anyway, they operated on my right leg and put rods into my femur bone. Once again I begged, 'Baba don't you think that my time has come? I want to unite with You, as well as Alok, because I am really tired of all this.' After being in hospital for about a fortnight, I came out only to find that my sister-in-law, who was my soulmate and companion, was admitted in hospital. She had been more of a mother to Alok than me as, physically, I had never been able to take care of him. In 2007, we came to know that she was suffering from breast cancer and three years later we came to know the cancer had spread rapidly. Here again, Baba was taking away my biggest life support.

After fighting a battle for her life, she was brought home to be with the family. Here she was, just fifty-six years of age, and knew that she was dying but all she said to everyone was, 'Take care of Charu once I am gone.' On 2nd June 2011, we lost her. There are times when one's faith is being built up, when one is being pushed to a stage of total surrender, and then at the very end, every form of human support is taken away. Possibly, this is what was occurring in my life at this time.

In the first year after Alok passed away, he came several times in my dreams. One day, I dreamt that I was teaching him Math and he kept telling me not to teach him Math but to read the Bhagvad Gita. Then he adds, 'Kyun vyarth chinta karte ho?' (Why do you fret unnecessarily?). That is when I knew that Alok probably wanted me to read the Gita. So I started reading a translation of it.

I began asking myself questions like, 'Who am I?' 'What is the purpose of my life?' And slowly, with the passage of time, I began to see how my faith was being tested and how surrender was the only answer.

If one looks at me, I am more like a vegetable. I can only talk or look at someone. I need to be helped for every need of mine. If I am not fed food, I'd probably just starve. I really sometimes wonder 'Why am I actually here?' The last thought that always comes to my mind is, 'What are we going to take from this world?' And yet again, all I can say to my Master is, 'Thank you for this awareness.'

The courage and strength that Meher Baba has now given me has actually helped me tide over every physical and emotional obstacle. Baba has also given me a lot of patience. I have now been on bed for the past eight months. I have not been outside the four walls of my room. After two major surgeries, I can't even bend my knees anymore. I may never put my feet on the floor. But I still feel mentally secure and I can say one thing: 'I have no fears at all about anything.'

This is only because Meher Baba has been coming repeatedly in messages and saying that, 'I'm by your side.' He has been sending His own people to come into my life to take care of me. Being connected to Baba leaves me with such a positive feeling that Baba is taking care of me and He is never going to leave me alone. Despite all the suffering, I am being looked after so well.

I started this story by saying what Alok felt when he was leaving this world. And I can actually say I'm a very proud mother that he felt like that! So I end this with the same words again: 'I love God – I love Baba – and I love you all very much.'

CHAPTER 16

Writings on the Wall

They say that walls have ears, but have you ever heard of a wall that can talk? Maybe when you come to Meherabad next time and stay at the Meher Pilgrim Retreat, you will take a look at the beautiful Tile Wall there and see what I mean.

It was 1995. *Sounds of Silence* had just been published and Meena Sisodia from Pune called to have a word with me.

The story of Karl had touched her deeply and it was the beginning of a new friendship, which was to take a dramatic turn a few years later. Our meetings lasted only for a while for Meena and her family soon relocated to New Zealand and I lost touch with her. Then, a decade later, in January 2005, I was really happy to hear her voice on the phone again. She told me that for some inexplicable reason she had picked up the book, begun reading it again, remembered old times and felt motivated to call me.

Another call followed a few days later to let me know that she had a small heart problem and was going in for an angioplasty. However, there was nothing in her voice or her manner of speaking which prepared me for what followed.

Two days later a strange, very broken voice informed me that in the process of the surgery Meena had passed away. The call was from her dear husband Chuck – and, of course, I could well imagine what he was going through! In the course of the conversation he told me that in the last few days, Meena had kept *Sounds of Silence* close to her heart all the time, and for some reason of her own, had insisted that he and their two children also promise to read it.

Chuck Sisodia

Meena and Chuck were both already very aware about spirit communication and had earlier decided that they would communicate with each other when the time came. *Sounds of Silence* paved the way for them.

Chuck was keen to go to Meherabad and take Baba's blessing before he gave it more serious thought, so a trip was arranged. He flew down from New Zealand and I met Chuck Sisodia for the first time on 2nd July 2005. To say he was charming is putting it mildly and he soon had all the ladies in our group running circles around him, doing their best to make him happy.

Yes, the obvious question was asked, 'Dearest Meena, will you be there for me, and how will I know you?' Chuck had several interesting experiences on his first trip to the Samadhi and this was when life changed for him. However, the second trip to Meherabad was amazing. So much occurred during this visit that I feel compelled to share it with you.

It was in April 2006 that Chuck was to visit Meherabad again. This time he was joining a small group that included me and two other ladies from Mumbai. Chuck could not resist asking the same question once again: 'Dear Meena – will you be there for me, and how will I know you?'

This time there was a message from her, which said: 'Meherabad is just a stone's throw away from the spot that I wish you to visit. It is on the hill next to the Samadhi that is where the new Centre lies. There you will find a piece of furniture that will trigger a memory for you. That memory I hold very dear to me. Look for it Chuck and when you find it, I shall be there by your side holding your hand and looking at it with you.

Many happy returns my Love – your Meena.'

Chuck being new to this sort of thing, I spent some time explaining to him that when the message speaks of 'being there by his side etc.,' it does not necessarily mean that he would actually see her in flesh and blood but that, definitely, her spirit would be close to him and a touch of the hands was also a distinct possibility.

As usual, after paying homage to Baba at the Samadhi, we wandered around the grounds and drove up to the new Centre as indicated in the message. But there was no one there except the caretaker who told us that it was only going to open in June. So we wandered around looking for some furniture, trying our best to help Chuck in his search. To our disappointment, we found the verandas empty, all the doors and windows shut, the reception and dining room closed, and the living rooms locked. It was a hot April afternoon. Not a leaf stirred, not a soul in sight, no place to sit, nothing for us to see or do. Now what? Every room was closed and there was not a single piece of furniture to be seen.

We were strolling aimlessly around the courtyard when suddenly a few wrought iron chairs caught our attention. They were scattered haphazardly near a beautiful tiled wall that ran the length of the open, stone-paved patio adjacent to the dining room. Chuck's eyes lit up. He pointed to the first chair in the corner and with quickening interest said, 'Oh! That is something Meena wanted for our patio.'

Suddenly one of the ladies called out to Chuck and exclaimed, 'Look, look Chuck! Come here, here is your message.' She held his hand and pointed to the beautiful tiled wall that surrounded us. There, staring right at us, was written in big bold letters, 'Welcome To My World.'

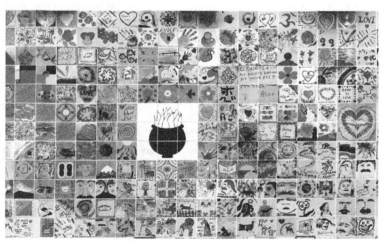

A section of the artistic Tile Wall.

Some of the selected messages on individual tiles.

As we read the last couple of lines, it took only a moment for each and every one of us to understand what was the miracle happening here. Some of us were choked with emotion, some shed silent tears. We slowly moved away, leaving Chuck to read and absorb the all-important lines on his own. That was all he really needed to know; Meena was with Baba and would always be there waiting for him.

As if this was not enough, as Chuck walked along the wall wondering if he was dreaming all this, another tile caught his eye. This one had a heart and 'CHUCK M' written on it.

To Chuck it was no longer a dream; it had become a reality. A small piece of furniture had led him to the place where his beloved had shown him that her spirit still lives on. The writings on the beautiful Tile Wall jogged his memory because the lines were from an old song that Meena and Chuck had loved; always sharing many such old songs together.

Those beautiful words are still there on that Tile Wall for all to see. I guess they will have a different meaning for different people. But for Chuck it made all the difference to his present life. That is how Baba always works. It all seems so simple, yet it remains an unforgettable experience for the heart that it is meant to touch.

Every year when Chuck now visits India, he makes it a point to go to Meherabad. Both his children have also visited with him. Whenever he goes, he never fails to sit there again and relive those few miraculous moments near that beautiful wall of tiles, especially painted by Baba lovers from all over the world.

He is in regular touch with Meena through Karl and, in this way, the love that flows through her shows him Baba's Love. He feels as close to his wife now, as he was when she was physically with him. Their love affair carries forward and he waits for the day when they will be united – listening to heavenly music together, again.

His love for Baba has also grown over the years. He says, 'Without Baba and Karl, I don't know how I would have handled my loss. For me it is a miracle. I have surrendered my life to Baba. His Will is my life. Materialistic things have no value anymore. I am happy with whatever Baba gives me because I know my pain is His pain, and my happiness is His happiness. Meena gave me so much love and taught me the meaning of love and now all I have is love to share.'

There are many different kinds of writing on Baba's wall of love, and there are different ways in which Baba reaches out to you and brings you to His doorstep.

Aparajita Banerjee

A young girl at a boarding school in Nainital was shedding bitter tears of rejection and loneliness, as it was now a long time since she had received a letter from home. She could not put her mind to studies and stayed aloof from the other girls until one night, as she lay crying in bed, she had a vision. She saw a beautiful Being clothed in light coming towards her. He was holding a crystal bowl with some liquid in it. He gently held the bowl to her lips and as she drank from it, she found the taste sweet and soothing. The memory of that taste still lingers in her mouth.

That little girl was I, Jita Banerjee, and since that day I have been searching for my 'Divine Beloved' and this is how I found Him.

A few months earlier, Nan's two books, *Sounds of Silence* and *Listening to the Silence* had touched my very soul and reawakened an almost 'ancient' spiritual yearning to 'reconnect' with my Divine Beloved, and heal an inexplicable, lifelong ache deep in my heart.

It is said that if you take just one loving step towards the Divine, He completes the journey Himself. During a weekend visit to Mumbai in December 2011 to meet my old school friend Villie, we were invited over by her friend Hilla who, it turned out, knew Nan and gave me her number. So when I came back to Pune, my dear friend Joan and I went to visit Nan who, after listening very patiently to my ramblings, said she would ask Karl how I may connect to my Divine Beloved. The very next day, Nan sent me a message from Karl ...

'Dearest Jita,

Your Divine Beloved is the Almighty – and He is at your service all the time. He loves you so much that He came to you when you were troubled and unhappy. For Him it was a pleasure to see you react to His love. It touched His heart. Now you have got this chance to make a personal connection with Him – Do it, and know that you will profit greatly by the event. It is now up to you to follow the leads God has given you to enter His heart and His home. He wants very much to see again that loving smile you gave Him so long ago.

That is the time He gave you a sip from the nectar of the Gods – something which has remained with you for a lifetime – just like His love. He will always and always be there for you. Now, how you keep up the connection with Him and how you progress on your path is all in your power and up to you Jita. Baba waits for you.

Love Karl.'

I felt so very blessed by this message. A week later, on 11th January 2012, Joan, Ulka, and I made the journey to Meherabad. I called Nan for any 'words of wisdom' she might have but she just said, 'Baba loves fun – go and enjoy yourself.' Baba's Samadhi was not very crowded that day and we were able to sit inside for some time. I poured my heart out to Baba and asked, 'Where is my Divine Beloved?' As I meditated, I felt as if a beautiful brass incense burner was circling my inner spiritual heart, purifying and blessing me. I once again opened the book of prayers and read the three special ones again. Finally, I came out feeling content and peaceful, that I had finally surrendered my spiritual yearnings to the One who understood.

I saw a nice lady was sitting on the bench outside. As soon as she heard that this was our first visit, she introduced herself as Bapsi and offered to show us around. She took us around Upper and Lower Meherabad. Everyone was so welcoming and kind, it was like being in a place where one truly belonged; where a Loved One had been patiently awaiting our arrival.

But for me the life changing moment arrived when sitting down there she read out Baba's Universal Message to me. She read it out loud till the end when I heard Baba declare, *'I am the Divine Beloved who loves you more than you can ever love yourself ... I am the Ancient One.'*[1] I was stunned. And my mind went numb in disbelief. Just half an hour earlier I had been praying to Meher Baba and seeking His guidance to find the one I call my Divine Beloved – I had got my answer. I had found my Divine Beloved.

From that moment on, I kind of moved on 'auto-pilot' for the rest of the day. I really cannot comprehend how Beloved Baba made me realise deep down that the Divine Beloved I was searching for since childhood – the One Who made me drink the nectar of God – was none other than God Himself in the form of Avatar Meher Baba.

I not only heard those blessed words, but Baba in His own inimitable way led me to a tile on the 'Wall of Love,' which said in swirling letters, 'Divine Beloved.' What more could I ask for?

CHAPTER 17

The Pune Circle

Both my books, *Sounds of Silence* and *Listening to the Silence*, had been out in the bookstores for some time and they had generated a lot of interest. A small group of believers had already formed and was growing steadily in Pune. A lot of academic questions about Baba – His life, work, and messages were being asked. My niece Zia Cama, when she was living in Mumbai, had attended many sessions of the Study Circle conducted every Tuesday by Cyrus Khambata at Baba's Bombay Centre, and she had learned much from them. While there was some talk of her relocating to Pune, she had been nurturing the idea of requesting Cyrus if he could conduct a similar book-reading session at her residence in Pune. This idea was received with great enthusiasm and unanimous approval by the newly-formed group of enthusiastic Baba lovers, and so an invitation went out to Cyrus and his wife Soumya. We were delighted when they accepted. That's how the fortnightly weekend sessions began in Pune and many of our questions got answered. The sessions were not only educative but also very lively and entertaining since they were interactive. What's more, Cyrus would invariably weave Baba-anecdotes and humour into the sessions to drive home a point.

The book reading started with Baba's *Discourses*. It is a fabulous book and I would recommend you to read it because not only will it expand your horizon, it will also guide you step-by-step into various aspects of life and love. The book touches upon various emotions most of us go through in life, their genesis and, in case of a disturbing pattern, the possible solutions. In short, the general guidelines for handling life's situations with equanimity and grace are embraced within its pages. Simply put, *Discourses* is a manual for living.

Starting from the very first session, most of us got so charged that we barely got through a page and the rest of the time went in asking questions that poured from all the fifteen or more members gathered there. Cyrus had to literally put up his hand to stem the barrage.

Before answering any question, Cyrus would invariably state that whatever he says is in accordance with his own level of understanding and interpretation of Baba's words, and that others may have their own viewpoint or opinion on the subject. Also, whenever he would quote Baba from memory, he would say that these may not be His exact words, but they are 'words to the effect.' He said they generally convey the sense and meaning behind Baba's words. Although Cyrus states this as a matter of abundant precaution, the group found that when he quoted Baba, he almost always quoted correctly.

———————

Q. In the beginning of Discourses, Baba says: 'As in all great critical periods of human history, humanity is now going through the agonising travail of spiritual rebirth. Great forces of destruction are afoot and seem to be dominant at the moment, but constructive and creative forces that will redeem humanity are also being released through several channels. Although the working of these forces of light is chiefly silent, they are eventually bound to bring about those transformations that will make the further spiritual advance of humanity safe and steady. It is all part of the divine plan, which is to give to the hungry and weary world a fresh dispensation of the eternal and only Truth.'![1]

What does that mean? The world seems to be in absolute chaos and actually going from bad to worse; is this the way it will always be? Or does Baba think that things will change?

Cyrus: Baba does not think, He knows ...

Being the source of Infinite Knowledge, He knows that all will be well and fine in the end. He gives us an analogy of Himself as the author of the novel titled *Creation*. He obviously knows what is written therein – being the author Himself – and He also knows how it will all end. And so Baba assures and reassures us time and again, *'Don't worry, be happy,'* that everything is in perfect order, that all is under His benevolent control and that there is going to be a happy ending for everyone and everything in creation. The in-between chapters in this novel *Creation* do seem unpalatable, even brutal and horrendous. But this is only a passing phase of experience to reach to the end of the novel, which has a happy and blissful ending. Believing in Baba's words buffers and cushions the reading of the in-between chapters, which translates into the actual life experiences which humanity is going through right now in this *kalyug* where chaos and, apparently, out-of-control situations reign supreme.

Baba says that all that we experience in the external world is actually an illusion – a dream, although it may appear to be real. A dream becomes a dream only upon waking up. As long as we are dreaming, the experience seems real. This external nightmare is to quicken the process of our awakening from the dream of illusion to the true nature of the Self and thus realign our values and priorities in life. To achieve that, Baba lays emphasis on loving Him, remembering Him and making Him our constant companion. The more we remember Baba with love and faith, the more we perceive and experience the falsity and the impermanence of the external world with all its experiences; and the quicker we emancipate ourselves from its grip by refining our perceptions of the apparently gruesome world.

Having said that, it should not be construed that Baba advocates only apathy or a callous attitude towards life. On the contrary, He exhorts us to hone our acumen and act as best as we can in any given circumstance to 'straighten up' what needs to be done; but with the clear understanding that all this is illusion, so that we cease to be attached to or affected by it, leaving the results to Baba. Baba expects us to shoulder all responsibilities, discharge all duties, face all worldly situations bravely and kindly, with enthusiasm and cheer, and maintain equipoise under all illusory circumstances.

In the *Discourses*, Baba speaks about the emergence of the 'New Humanity' that will come about through the dispensation of Divine Love that will bring about an end to all competition, conflict and rivalry. It will break itself free from the tyranny of and attachment to dead forms of external rites, rituals, ceremonies, traditions and conventions, which in most cases fetters the release of the life of the spirit.

So, coming back to your question, yes, good times are ahead for sure, but the workings of these positive forces are chiefly silent and underground.

Our Pune group, which ranged between ten to twenty members at any given session, comprised of doctors, teachers, healers, psychoanalysts and, of course, home-makers. The questions kept pouring in session-after-session on diverse issues. Many of us took notes of all that was explained concerning the readings, as well as the answers given by Cyrus to our perennial flow of questions. During these last five years, we have covered *Discourses, God Speaks* and *Beams from Meher Baba on the Spiritual Panorama, The Everything and The Nothing,* and now we are on to *The Path of Love.* These sessions continue even today.

From the various questions asked from time to time, I am giving here only a few for the benefit of readers.

Q. We are told that everything happens according to the Will of God; how are we to know what is God's Will? Besides, if everything is as per God's Will, what is the sense in making any effort? It is all so complicated and confusing.

Cyrus: In order to understand rationally this enigmatic question, we need to look at one of Baba's profound statements: Baba says: *'My Will is Law, My Wish governs the Law and My Love sustains the universe.'[2]* The statement – My Will is Law – connotes that God's Will is actualised and expressed through the operation of His Law – the Law of Cause and Effect, popularly known as the Law of Karma. It is a binding Law and it operates on all of creation. Its dominion is over the domain of illusion. It does not and cannot, however, touch the ones who are free from illusion – ones who are established in the Truth – the Realised Ones.

The Law is impartial and inexorable; it knows no concessions, gives no preferences, and makes no exceptions. It works meticulously with exactitude. It is an expression of justice and a reflection of the unity of all life in the world of duality. The manner of operation of this Law cannot be fully intelligible as long as the gross body and the gross world are considered to be the only facts of existence. It operates even in the disincarnate afterlife states of so-called Heaven and Hell, during the process of reincarnations, in the incarnate state of a human; right up to the end of involution – a step before Realisation.

From this one can see that God, in His infinite wisdom, has programmed such a Law where automatically one is punished not 'for' his deeds but 'by' his deeds. And the Law holds true for both, the vicious as well as the virtuous. This automatic operation of the Law ensures the resultant punishment and reward life after life with absolute precision. All this leads us to understand that, in a sense, God does not do anything but His Will governs the creation through the operation of His Law. In this sense nothing happens without the Will of God.

To illustrate: A king has passed a law that states, among other things, that those who are caught stealing would be jailed, and those found guilty of murder would be hanged. Many of his subjects must have received such punishments in accordance with this law of the land, which is nothing but the king's will. The king himself may not even be aware of the details of punishments meted out, and yet it can be said that everything that happens in his kingdom is as per the king's will.

The feeling prevalent among the masses that the wicked are enjoying life while the virtuous are suffering, is a result of ignorance of the Law of Karma coupled with a narrow, key-hole vision limiting life only to its physical manifestation.

Q. What then is destiny and what is its relationship to fate or luck? Is it true that our destinies are predetermined? If so, who decides our destiny and on what basis is it determined for each individual? If everything is as per destiny then where is the place of free will in the whole scheme of things?

Cyrus: Let us first try to understand, with our limited intellect, creation and its grand purpose. Baba says, **'God alone is Real and all else that seems real is an illusion – a dream.'**[3] Therefore, the whole of creation is unreal – an illusion, but a significant one. The purpose of creation is to awaken us – each drop-soul – from the dream of illusion to the realisation of the Truth. In that sense, the universe is like a Divine incubator in which the consciousness of the soul incubates and evolves till it is full and complete in the first human form, whereafter through the recurrent process of reincarnation, and involution, it reaches the Divine goal of Realisation. In that sense, destiny is the Divine Law of Will, which guides each drop-soul from the beginning of evolution to the ultimate goal of Realisation. Hence, destiny is one and the same for all – the Realisation of Truth.

Another one of Baba's beautiful statements which corroborates the above thought, is: **'There is no creature that is not destined** *for the supreme goal, even as there is no river that is not on its winding way to the ocean.'*[4] Hence, whether we like it or not, want it or not, we are all destined to reach our destiny – the supreme goal. The winding of the river – this way or that – is the means, process or pathway chosen by the river to arrive at and merge with the ocean, which may be called its free will, which, incidentally, is circumscribed between the two banks and generally follows the path of least resistance.

In like manner, fate or luck is the means or process of expending, utilising, experiencing and balancing the accumulated past sanskaras or impressions that one has gathered through the travails of evolution, reincarnation and involution. It is the automatic operation of the Law of Karma based on past actions. Baba gives the simile of every soul having to bear a burden of seven hundred tons – a certain amount of suffering and happiness – throughout its evolution, reincarnation and involution, right up to Realisation. The weight is the same for all, but the kind and form of weight varies in accordance with the lives lived in the past and resultant sanskaras gathered. Thus the soul's present experiencing of past sanskaras, through the automatic operation of the Law, means fate or luck. Since the sanskaras of different drop-souls are different, their experience – what we call fate or luck – varies. So destiny is one and the same for all, but fate or luck is different.

From the standpoint of ultimate Truth, however, the so-called free will is only apparent. A cow tied on a long rope pegged to a post may consider herself completely free to move wherever she desires, but in truth her movements are confined within the circumference prescribed by the length of the rope. She may experience this as freedom but in actuality it is not so. Likewise, our apparent free will is in accordance with the working out of our own sanskaras, which drive us to take a certain course of action rather than the other. Thus our so-called free will is operative within the ambit of God's Will, meaning only if supported by God's Will.

Although in Truth there is no such thing like free will, Baba, I believe, expects us to act *as if* there is free will as evident from this profound message given by Him in the *Discourses*: *'Fate, however, is not some foreign and oppressive principle. Fate is man's own creation pursuing him from past lives; and just as it has been shaped by past karma, it can be modified, remoulded and even undone through karma in the present life ... Proper understanding and the use of the law of karma enables man to become master of his own destiny through intelligent and wise action.*[5]

So, one can see here the role of free will, howsoever seeming or apparent it may be from the standpoint of Truth. Looking at it from yet another ángle, what comes on the screen of our consciousness as an experience, event, happening, occasion, occurrence etc. is the result of our past karma – fate, luck, *taqdeer, naseeb,* loosely also called destiny – which is inescapable and unchangeable. How we respond to it is our free choice. In that sense, the present moment – the eternal now – is the meeting point between the predetermined fate and the free will.

Baba further elucidates that according to the Vedantists and the Sufis, God does everything. That is the truth, no doubt, but being short of the actual experience behind the assertions, it would be hypocritical to say so. Such assertions based on ignorance of knowledge, on mere reasoning and logic, could lead to terrible consequences.

For example, Baba says, *'You and I are not we but one.'* From Baba's standpoint – the standpoint of truth – it is a fact, the absolute truth, but being short of the experience, I cannot assert 'Baba and I are one.' And so, as long as we are in the domain of illusion, I feel, it would be prudent to keep exercising our so-called free will in a spiritually intelligent manner so that we use the Law of Karma to help emancipate us from the bondage of illusion.

Q. But what about the suffering that entails one simply because one is born unluckily under a certain nakshatra or zodiac?

Cyrus: I believe that each zodiac has its own energy, specialty and distinctiveness, and a soul arrives on earth on that particular day and at that specific time when the celestial rays are in mathematical harmony with one's individual karma. Therefore, when one experiences the ups and downs in life, it is not because one is born under a particular sign; on the contrary, it is because one has 'chosen' to be born under that particular sign – due to his past karma – so as to afford the consciousness of the soul the best possible avenue to experience, utilise and balance its past karmas. When we say 'chosen' it is an automatic and involuntary choice, in accordance with the Law of Karma, where the sanskaras gravitate or impel the soul to take form on that particular day and at that specific time.

The horoscope, if cast and read correctly, is only a portrait revealing the unalterable past, and maps out its probable future. But one need not slavishly be attached to it for, just as we have produced the film of our present life through past karma, we have the power and the authority to edit it, through corrective actions in the present, for a better film of our life in the future.

It is therefore wise to accept every experience in life as the harvest of the seed self-sown in the past, with a clear understanding that no experience comes to the consciousness of the soul unless such an experience is needed to express the impressed sanskaras on our consciousness. In other words, to utilise and balance out the earlier impressions – experiencing them is inevitable. And in that sense, there is no such thing as 'unlucky' or 'negative' since any so-called negative experience is nothing but the fruit of our past sowing and, if accepted with equanimity and responded with spiritually prudent action, it reverses and balances the earlier impression. So it is a win-win situation – what really matters is how we look at it.

CHAPTER 18

Hold On

Baba often exhorts His followers, *'Hold on to My daaman with both hands.'*[1] What does it mean in practical terms?

It could mean so many things; to stick to Him through the so-called good and bad times – the illusory rollercoaster of our lives, to have full and complete faith in Him, depending on Him for every little thing in our life by remembering Him, making Him our constant companion, trusting Him wholly and surrendering all our strengths and weaknesses to Him. When we keep holding on to His daaman – the hem of the garment, we inevitably follow Him wherever He goes. Figuratively, it implies that we follow His wish, live His message of love, truth and unity of all life. In short, to conduct our lives in a manner that would not only glorify Him but will also please Him.

In Baba's words: *'Now I will explain about holding fast to My daaman. Hold Me, or leave Me! Do not try to compromise. One thing is definite and fixed: if I am the Highest of the High or if I am the Lowest of the Low, and you hold fast to My daaman, you will be where I will be. This depends on how fast is your grip on My daaman. It matters not if you are saints or sinners.*

I will give you one example. In My boyhood, I liked very much to fly kites. You know that kites have long tails and as they soar high in the skies, the tails flutter vigorously. If they hold fast to the kite, they go where the kite flies. It matters little whether the tails are stuck with fine gum or some dirty thing. What is needed is that the grip should not loosen. In the same way, whether you are sinners or saints, if you hold fast to My daaman, you will be wherever I will be.'[2]

Painting of Meher Baba flying a kite with a happy child.

Having said that, it is the experience of quite a few who have strayed on account of their weakness, ignorance, non-fulfillment of their desires or anything else, that during the period of their so-called dissociating or distancing from Baba, it was Baba who held on to them and brought them back into His fold.

Now listen to what Raynah Tayabali has to say ...

Raynah Tayabali

I had surrendered to Baba in the 1990s. At least that is what I told Baba. Nevertheless, in 2005, I met a Guru who I was told was a great healer. I needed healing for my knee, so I got in touch with him and joined as one of his *sadhaks*. However, I continued going to Meherabad once a year and acknowledged Baba as being my God. I will refer to this Guru as 'the guru' for the rest of this story. I experienced many things during those years with the guru. I saw people being healed. I also learnt to do specific types of *sadhanas*, chant mantras, worship and wear certain *yantras*. I experienced things I had never experienced before during meditation and I think my ego was too caught up in what I was experiencing. The guru did say that 'unconditional love' was the most important thing and I tried to follow that.

By the end of 2009, it seemed as though this phase of my life had come to a close and there was a feeling of anticipation. It felt as if I was on a diving board ready to take a plunge. 2010 began with a long holiday for me and I returned to Mumbai on the 12th of March. Three days later, I met with an accident that was the turning point in my life. I was knocked down by a speeding motorbike and lay unconscious, bleeding, bruised, and with an arm broken in several places. I was taken to a nearby Nursing Home. Later, my sister told me that a young boy by the name of Ritvick had brought me there and that he had come with his mother and met her. The nurse had also told me that it was fortunate I was brought in when I was because I was bleeding profusely from the head and a delay may have resulted in more complications and perhaps may have proved fatal. So I really owed very much to this young lad. My sister had also told me that Ritvick was a follower of the guru, and this touched me profoundly. It was not by chance that this young boy was nearby.

I spent two months now with my family as earlier I used to live alone. During this time, Nan Umrigar had her book launch in Mumbai and I missed it. I was eager to read her new book *Listening to the Silence*. In May, I was back at my own place of residence. I had bought a copy of *Listening to the Silence* and started reading it. I remember the day, 11th May 2010, and what followed is etched in my memory in vivid detail.

I was reading about Don Stevens and how Baba embraced him, not once but several times. I then wished I would be embraced by Baba like that. No sooner did I have the thought then, seemingly coming out of that very page, I sensed an energy enveloping and embracing me over and again. I started crying. It was so exquisitely wonderful to be held like that and all the pain of what had happened to me vanished. I felt whole.

But Baba was not content with just that. He wanted to make sure I got the message. That night, I awoke to be greeted by the strong fragrance of Baba's favourite flower that filled the room. The next day on my way in a rickshaw to the Nursing Home for an X-ray, as I passed the place where the accident had taken place, I saw an image of Baba on a bike going at full speed, his hair blowing in the wind. Hallucination? Maybe. But that was the moment I let go of my resentment for the hit-and-run driver who had knocked me over.

In June 2011, I went to Meherabad to thank Baba and ask His forgiveness. I knew that something had changed in me, but I was still struggling between following the practices of meditation I had learnt from the guru, and just being with and listening to Meher Baba. At that time, I received a message through Karl telling me that Baba had forgiven me. It took me some time to realise the enormity of my actions; of having strayed from Baba and allowing my ego to take over; of having moved away from the Avatar, the very source of all holiness, to seek holiness elsewhere. There was one line in Karl's message that stood out for me, although I did not fully understand it then. It read: *'Your footsteps are once more mirrored in the sands of time.'*

That was not the end of the story. Baba, so to speak, had the last laugh. Months later, I wanted to get in touch with Ritvick and, as his telephone number had changed, I went to his house. I wanted to take him some CDs with discourses of the guru. Fortunately I did not, for my sister had got it wrong. When I reached his house, on the landing outside his door, I saw a picture of Meher Baba. I was stunned. All this time, I was under the impression that Ritvick, who had been instrumental in saving my life, was a follower of the guru. Here, God Almighty Himself was staring down at me. I walked into a Baba home. I met Ritvick's mother, Richa Sharad, his aunt Neha Sharad, and Ritvick himself.

The young lad narrated what had happened: how he had difficulty getting me into a rickshaw, how he had threatened to hit the driver when he resisted; how people wanted to call the police, but not get involved themselves, etc. I was thinking of the image of the biblical David who had knocked over the mighty Goliath with a stone. Baba indeed was the stone. He was there from start to finish. What I have gained from all of this is a deep experience of a faithful God who loves us, no matter what. I have no time to waste now on other gurus. Baba is the way, the truth, the life, and love ... and I need nothing else.

Reaching Beyond

Since we have been talking about questions, the most common questions I am asked are: 'Can you please give us an overall picture of what happens to the soul on passing? In your experience what are the salient features? How does auto writing help? How does it work? Does it only enable you to communicate with the higher world, or does it confer any other benefits on the person who is writing?'

In the cycle of life, we are born as a baby, soon become a child, then a teenager who grows into an adult, and then after we become old and aged, the body dies. But after we die, what happens to us? What happens is that we go one step beyond. We shed the aged form, and enter the spirit world. But, just because we do not have a physical body anymore, we do not stop growing.

According to the Masters, by the time we arrive into the spirit world, we have already lived a life, maybe gone through some physical pain like an illness or some emotional trauma. It could be a life cut short by an accident, or just a body that has died due to old age. Whatever the case may be, the first thing that happens when we reach the spirit world is that we enter a stage of renewal. We go through a period of rest that normally lasts for approximately ninety days. The length of this rest period varies from person to person. Some are ready to move on faster, while others need a longer time to get accustomed to the fact that they are no longer in their physical bodies. The more one's attachment to the physical world, either in the form of people or material possessions, the longer is the adjustment period. The Masters also say that this is a learning stage where we are shown our whole life as a movie. We are then guided by our spirit helpers, our family guides and our Masters who help us see how we handled the life we had chosen; if we did it all correctly or where we had gone astray. They help us find the right answers so that they remain in our subconscious mind and become a source that we can tap into the next time around if, and when, we face the same situations again. This is not a time when we are judged harshly for what we have done wrong. The Masters are Beings of love and they gently guide us through the process. We witness each event, no matter how minor, in this unique manner. There is no judgement – but a replay of our lives lived in totality.

This is an important learning time to understand how we have touched others, or how they have influenced our lives. We experience every encounter, every relationship; we see whom we have helped or whom we have hurt; whom we have loved and whom we have hated. This period not only helps us to review the life we have just left behind, but it also helps us to plan for the next one. It helps us decide when, where and for what reason we want to return; to choose our parents, our friends and relationships. It helps us to heal and it helps us to plan our future destiny. It helps us to understand that our physical body is transient, and it is only the soul and the spirit that is eternal. Therefore during this vital period of learning and rest, the soul should not be disturbed.

My writings are all based on Love – Love of God, love of those who have passed on, as well as those who are waiting to connect. Auto writing is the art of contacting other intelligences through the use of pen and paper, while in an altered or meditative state of consciousness. There are normally three types of contacts or connections you can make. You can either contact your higher Self, other loving entities, or your own spirit guide.

I have been auto writing almost every single day for twenty-seven years and it has brought me joy and happiness beyond compare. It is incredible how much I have begun to understand, and how it has led me on to the spiritual path. It has not only brought me to Meher Baba and kept me in touch with my beloved husband Jimmy, and my son Karl; it has also brought thousands of other people into Baba's fold. I have taken them to the Samadhi, helped them find solutions to their problems, and given them a reason to live on even after they have encountered great tragedies along the way. To be able to face life with joy following a devastating incident in one's personal life, is the real answer to living. I feel greatly honoured to be given the gift of helping people achieve this.

I am very aware that when He was in the world, Baba had certain reservations about His followers connecting with the spirit world, and people becoming attached to the occult. He thought that it was really not necessary. But He also assured the world that, *'The Powerhouse will never fail provided the wires maintain their connection with it,'*[1] and I do keep that always in mind. So, I do not ever encourage young or emotionally disturbed people to start on it as a regular exercise, for it sometimes draws one away from reality and keeps one engrossed with the unknown. It makes one dependent on what is going to be instead of what is, and one stops making choices for oneself. That is not what the writing is for. It is there for us to get to know more about God, how He functions, and how He loves. It is for us to know that even if our loved ones have passed on, they still can keep contact with us and help us from that side. It is totally up to us how we draw our energy from that powerhouse and make it available to mankind.

Karl says:

'Baba wants to make many more friends in the world and that is why your work is increasing in size and value. But do not worry, He will not give you more than you can handle and that is why He is reaching out to more people who can auto write and so make a greater effort to help others.

It is a way of making more people believe in the Love of God, to profit by His mercy, and to understand the language of the heart rather than to go with the dictates of the mind. This is just one more way of making the world a better place to be in, where human beings feel blessed to receive the bounty of God and to make their way forward in peace. It is one more way to prevent strife, to stop destruction, and to motivate the world to go forward towards the Light.

That is why this concept is spreading so fast, where more and more people want to make deeper contact with their Higher Selves instead of depending on their bodies.

I hope you can pass this on to those that understand why Baba has made inroads into this field of thought and is striving to make it a reality for so many.

Meher Baba is happy with your work. He is not at all bothered that we are using the writing to make a connection with those that have passed on. He knows that we have to do that because it is one of the ways in which Baba can make those that are sad feel better, as well as show people that the two worlds are not too far away from each other. Baba is sitting here and using this means to make a connection.

This is just one of Baba's ways of revealing Himself and of making people happy. For Baba, 'Real Happiness lies in making others Happy,' and by making a contact He is doing just that.'

There are many in the world who are now practicing auto writing and in doing so have had the opportunity of coming closer to their higher Self, being more relaxed, and leading a happier life. So, for the benefit of all those who are reading this, I will now give you a few testimonies from those who have already learnt to write and how they feel about it.

Behram Patel

Jai Meher Baba! Dear Nan Aunty,

Thank you very, very much for your and Karl's help once again. I am deeply satisfied with the auto writing I am doing with my spirit guide. It again brings me to realise what I had once read in a book long back; that it is the message that counts, and not the messenger.

In fact, when I look back now at all those times when I pressed my spirit guide to write much more, and even legibly, I realise the deeper reason and feel deeply sorry for pushing him too hard. Anyway whatever was done was done in ignorance and innocence.

Over the last four years that I have been writing, I have slowly passed the stage of asking anything to my spirit guide. Not asking and not expecting anything in return is really so much more satisfying. It is actually a different kind of a happiness that one slowly comes to experience over time. Auto writing has taught me so much that I am more than grateful for the scribbles that came through ever so often. It helped me to cultivate patience, acceptance, obedience, along with a sense of detachment and issues arising out of my ego. Most of all, it has helped me come closer to Baba and realise His worth.

My auto writing is progressing very well and I am so happy and content in continuing with it every day.

I thank the Divine Soul for its protection and strength throughout my life.

With lots of love,

Behram

Rupam Nangia

I read *Sounds of Silence* by Nan Umrigar over ten years ago. It was with considerable amazement and some disbelief that I learnt there could be any kind of communication between the spirit world and us. It became obvious to me that Karl's messages to his mother through automatic writing compelled her to seek Meher Baba, just as it compelled my family and me to seek Meher Baba as soon as we finished reading the book. Countless others, across the globe, have sought the blessings of the Master in Meherabad, thanks to the writings between Karl and his mother.

I lost my mother in 2010 and thus, grief-stricken and bereft of all contact with her, I felt the need to communicate with her. Having received many messages through Karl over the years, and with the knowledge that Meher Baba guided Karl in his mission, I requested Nan to initiate me in the art of automatic writing.

Six months after mom had left us, I started communicating with her through auto writing. Though I had understood the process and had been a witness to its simplicity and beauty, I was pleasantly surprised at the insightful and surreal experience it turned out to be! I learnt that my mother, father, and nephew were safe and happy in Baba's loving care and found that mom is at her eloquent best when she speaks of Baba and His compassionate and merciful ways! After a few weeks of drawing lines, designs and doodles, the first complete sentence she wrote was, 'Meher Baba is God.' This declaration came on its own as I had asked no questions and was not even expecting a coherent message on that day!

No words can describe my joy on reading those words on paper! I wanted to share them with the whole world! What I believed was now being corroborated by none other than my mom, from the other world! She sounded happy when describing her life and activities in her new home but her dominant theme, of late, has been the beauty and compassion of dear Baba. She exhorts my sisters and me to repose our complete faith and trust in Him. She counts herself fortunate that her prayers in several lifetimes have been answered and culminated in her reaching the holy feet of Meher Baba. An ardent devotee of Krishna in her lifetime, she found and recognised her Krishna in Baba and is overwhelmed by the beauty and purity of her experience!

These last few months have found me answering questions of relatives and friends – questions that are relevant and potent to them. Some have been guided to Meherabad to dear Baba's Samadhi. They have blossomed into Baba devotees. I have also recently been able to help a family connect with their dead son who was keen to communicate with his mother.

Auto writing has not just been a process of answering people's questions. It has opened a whole new world for me! Each of the writings, each encounter, and each counsel from mother has opened new vistas that I did not know existed! Her reluctance in answering mundane, material questions is evident and she reminds me ever so often that she is no astrologer! But ask her something about the spiritual realm, particularly where she can describe Baba and His greatness, and the flow of words is beautiful and unending!

I am beginning to understand more and more that Baba does everything with a purpose. His purpose in permitting us to pursue auto writing with our dear departed ones is, perhaps, to mitigate our fear of death; to tell us that the dividing line between the living and dead is thin; and to help these two worlds come closer. The most important lesson in it for me is that it is His Divine Will that shapes our life and our afterlife too.

Jai Meher Baba.

Renuka Alimchandani

My journey with Baba starts on a day when, almost accidentally, Nan Umrigar's *Sounds of Silence* fell in my lap. But then, there are no accidents or unplanned events in life. Reading this book was a powerful experience and it shook me to the depths. The night on which I finished the book, Baba appeared on the ceiling of my room as if announcing His arrival in my life.

Years later, I met Nan aunty through a common friend to seek help regarding my tumultuous life. Karl's answers to my queries and confusions brought me into Baba's fold and since then there has been no turning back.

It was during this time that Karl made me aware of my ability to do automatic writing. It all started with an unconscious tapping of my finger of the right hand, without any conscious effort on my part. The finger would start tapping by itself due to some unseen force. At first, I sought help from a psychiatrist but when no results came, I sought advice from Karl who told me it's a natural gift and that he himself will come and write with me if I so wish.

So I started with some usual precautions in place. Prayers for protection, and keeping Baba's photograph with a diya or candle burning before it. They say that all this helps to keep intruders at bay and ensures that only our guides come and communicate with us.

My experience with automatic writing has changed my life – from a dull and dreary one – to being the most powerful and beautiful experience. Karl's messages of Baba's Love and Grace have instilled a peace, unaffected by external circumstances, and have changed me as a person, and I have matured spiritually.

Apart from teaching me the basic qualities of tolerance, patience and empathy, Karl has made sure I follow a path of soul-searching and soul-growth rather than entertaining my inquisitiveness. From the beginning, he made it very clear – no foretelling the future and no materialistic queries. Needless to say, I followed his instructions.

Recently, with Baba's Grace and His instructions through Karl, I have started a blog, the main aim of which is to connect the spirit world and the earth by connecting loved ones on both the sides. It has brought many into Baba's fold and given hope to many inconsolable, grieving, loved ones on earth – as well as much peace to the departed loved ones on the other side.

For me, auto writing has become a way of connecting with my Master Meher Baba and experiencing His unconditional love and grace from above. It has enriched my life and transformed it into a journey worth living. It has guided me through the dark passages of my life and brought me much peace and comfort. I have found a friend, philosopher and guide in Karl, without whom I cannot imagine my life. His constant guidance and support have made decisions easy and put me on the path to Self-realisation, which would not have been possible, had it not been for automatic writing.

CHAPTER 20

A New Dawn, A New Life

I had a life-changing experience when I was just seventeen. I had a dear friend Mina who was in love with a boy who was addicted to drinks and drugs, and she was devastated. Having lived in a secure and loving family, I had never been exposed to the seamy side of life, so this was all really new for me. But there it was, and I could not get away from it.

I had just got my learner's driving license, so my friend would often beg me to drive her around so she could follow her boyfriend to see where he went, who he met, and what he did. It was rather horrible following him into some of the sleaziest places in Mumbai. He was visiting a doctor who was supplying him with some injections, which he had started taking on his own. We often used to find him passed-out in some by-lane and drag him out of his car, hide him till he was better, and then take him to his home.

Being exposed to all this was rather scary. I know what my friend went through – the lies, the cheating, his awful behaviour. Eventually, his family found out and sent him away to a Rehab centre abroad. He came back, married Mina, and they both lived happily ever after.

The memories of all that I had seen with Mina came back to my mind in 2010, when Sarita who lived in Nasik approached me one day for help.

I will let Sarita tell you her story, in her own words, about how Baba helped them.

Sarita Patil

Without it really having sunk in or maybe because I was unwilling to accept or admit it at the time, I had married a very charming and likeable man who had an extremely addictive personality. He was always the life of the party, and both young and old enjoyed his company. The fact that he was selfish and rather full of himself was obvious but the vices, and I mean *vices*, I assumed were just part and parcel of youth and would fade away in time. Wine, women, song, and much more were there for all to see. So were the lies, which come naturally to addicts. But, he was different, quite unlike anyone I had met before. Maybe that is what attracted me to him – he was the guy with a difference!

Our days of courting and early married life went by without much ado. We were like any newly married couple – very much in love and having a good time. Of course we had our ups and downs, and the stormy days, if and when they occurred, were weathered. We brought two gorgeous children into this world and they made our lives complete. Today I can proudly say that even in adversity, they have stood the test of time with their heads held high. They have pursued their dreams and been my pillars of strength all through. My two children, my lovely mother, and a dear friend, have been my anchor and support through a trying and testing period.

While my husband and I both pursued our respective careers with well-established companies, we still managed to live a rather active social life. Alcohol flowed at parties but by no means did it govern our lives.

Somewhere, at some time, my hands fell on *Sounds of Silence*. Not being an avid reader, but knowing the author and her family over some generations, made me curious to read the book. Both my children read it too. When you pick up this book to read, you simply cannot put it away till it's over. It's not something you would want to read in parts. Having closely monitored Karl's premature passing, from the moment of his accident to his untimely end, I could empathise with Nan's situation.

At social get-togethers, the conversation would at times stray to *Sounds of Silence* and Meherabad. Undoubtedly, there was a calling. One day, when my family and I were in a city close to Ahmednagar, a friend offered to accompany me to Meherabad. Attending the early morning aarti was a peaceful and calming experience. Everything around us was so serene. However, I was desperately looking for a sign, for a signal, to prove to me that Baba was there. I wondered why no butterfly flew and perched itself on my shoulder. Visiting Nan in Pune, hearing her stories, seeing Baba's face, which suddenly had appeared one day on a rock in her garden, was not enough proof for me. I needed to know for myself that Baba was there watching and listening to me.

Time went on and my husband decided to quit his job, and all the perks that went with it, to start his own business. He became his own boss and, in no time at all, discipline and routine went out of the window. That, to my mind, was when the landslide really began – pebble-by-pebble, stone by stone, rock by rock – my life came hurtling down. A few monetary gains came our way through gambling, but then huge setbacks followed. We were riding a dangerous and unstoppable roller coaster. It became obvious to me that alcohol and substance abuse had overtaken his thought process, his sensibility, and his whole life. He was often disoriented, behaved atrociously and the decline was very rapid. I stopped accompanying him on social outings, which I truly enjoyed, as I could not bear to see him make a fool of himself. People laughed openly at him, gossiped about him behind his back, while my husband appeared oblivious to it all or simply chose not to care and continued to make a fool of himself.

In desperation, I reached out to his family and friends for help. I did not get much support – partly disbelief and partly fear of losing him as a son, a brother, and a friend were, I imagine, the reasons for this rejection. At home, each day brought a rude awakening, and an even ruder ending. He insulted and mocked the kids; they could not bear to be at home until he went to bed and was fast asleep. There was no familial relationship. They were full of remorse and hatred; they wanted him out and tried to convince me that I had backed the wrong horse. Not many could digest his presence and those who did, probably had their own selfish reasons for putting up with him. From a warm and kind man, he had turned into a living monster. There was no normalcy in our lives. The moment he came home, all hell would break loose. There were also several tell-tale signs that he was engaged in liaisons with undesirable types. People would ask why I did not opt out of this madness, this situation that was ruining our lives.

Simply put, I could not. I knew it was a sickness, a disease, and that he needed help. How could I abandon him when he needed me the most? Taking him to a psychiatrist, which I tried, did not help. The prescribed medication was taken and discarded as he pleased. I was very clear that nothing short of a long-term rehabilitation would cure him.

In my desperate state, I had often toyed with the idea of sending a message to a departed soul. However, thus far, I had abstained. But things escalated and I desperately needed guidance from the Lord. I wrote to Nan, and she sent a message to Karl. His response arrived the very next day. Baba was now aware of the situation and assured me help, but there was just one thing I was asked to do. I had to take my husband to the Samadhi – just once, and then leave the rest to Baba. I felt a sense of complete hopelessness. How in a million years would I achieve this? Someone who was beyond reason or understanding, who was incommunicado at the best of times, who showed no signs of spirituality or faith in the Almighty – how could I get him to Meherabad? It was not very close to where I lived and, surely if it was to be, he would have accompanied me on one of my earlier trips.

Our relationship too had hit rock-bottom and on one occasion, whilst attempting to converse with him on how we should take things forward between the two of us, he actually suggested we go out of town and talk things through. Here was my chance and I grabbed it with both hands. I knew he had been waiting to go for a meeting, not far from Meherabad. So I engineered a trip and pleaded with him to accompany me to Meherabad, if only for a few minutes. He agreed to give it a thought. The impossible happened. We went together and his head touched the stone of Baba's Samadhi. Now it was truly in Baba's hands.

Nothing changed. Things only seemed to worsen. In June 2010, I wrote to Nan saying our lives were unbearable. Nan regrettably wrote back that only time would tell what Baba had in store. Chaos, trauma, fear governed our lives. The children would ensure that their room door was locked at all times, when their father was at home. They would pretend to be asleep if he knocked. I too would often pretend to be asleep because if he knew I was awake, he would start behaving obnoxiously. This would obviously lead to arguments and accusations. But I had to think of myself too. I had to get a few hours of sleep if there was half-a-chance of making it to work the next morning. So, I could only hope that he would be exhausted enough to hit the bed, in no mood to blast the music or the TV in our bedroom, or otherwise make a nuisance of himself, which he seemed to revel in doing at ungodly hours.

As much as I tried keeping my faith and hopes alive, I was fully aware I could not achieve this on my own. God knows I had tried. One day, a friend of my husband rang me out of the blue, wanting to meet immediately, as he heard my husband had gone too far. He was determined to help and I thought that, perhaps, my angel in disguise had arrived.

In a matter of days, we managed to fix an appointment with the doctor who owns a rehab clinic close to our city. This programme being voluntary, the person cannot be admitted against his or her wishes. So the doctor guided us as to how we should go about this. A plan was put into action: the family had to make sure he left the house and stay firm. Not something I would wish on anyone, but the doctor assured us that this was the only way, and within ten to fifteen days he would break and relent. We had to be ruthless and endure the outcome, whatever form it would take. The saying that you have to 'be cruel to be kind' buzzed around in my head. Minutes seemed like hours, and each day seemed like a lifetime, but there was no stopping us now. On Day 3, my husband messaged me saying he was on his way home and I could take an appointment with the doctor. Baba had worked His magic. Between the third and tenth day, when he eventually entered rehab, not for one moment did I lose faith or waver. Baba helped me stand steadfast, remain positive and make sure I saw this through for the sake of my husband and the rest of my family.

In October 2010 he entered rehab and, almost a year later, in November 2011, he returned home – a new man. Our pain and suffering is a thing of the past and we are now a close-knit family once again. My husband has come out a healed and better man; made new and lasting friends with whom he shares a great equation; forgiven himself, and forgiven me. A life has been saved; a family has been brought together. We are all taking tiny steps and trying to enjoy our time together, while we are learning to bond again. Trust is the most important aspect of any relationship and I hope, in time, I learn to trust again.

I wrote to Nan one more time and asked her to thank Baba and Karl; to tell them all was well and that I had my husband back and the children had their father. A gentle message came back to remind me that this was only the beginning and we had far to go. Karl's final message said that we should make one more trip to the Samadhi, especially on *Dhuni* day, and that my husband should accompany us. And so we did. This time there was no resistance from him. On 12th January 2012, my children, my husband and I visited Meherabad and we stayed the night at the Pilgrim Centre. We took part in the Dhuni proceedings and threw our weaknesses into the blazing fire. We attended the aarti in the evening and also the following morning. What really moved me was that, in spite of there being a long line of people waiting to go into the Samadhi, somehow Baba had made it possible that at one point we were the only four people present inside, not having to share the Divine space with another pilgrim or helper, which is very, very rare. I could not have imagined or hoped for this – the feeling was quite awesome. Baba had undoubtedly set this up for our family.

Whatever is to happen in the future, we know that we have made giant strides, achieved the impossible by keeping our faith and never losing sight of our goal, though it often appeared to take forever. Baba was only testing our patience and inner strength before He felt it was time to reward us. What I would like to share most, with some of you in a similar situation, is that determination, an indomitable spirit, and the power of faith can overcome even what destiny charts out for you. Life is what you make of it.

Jai Baba.

Conclusion

Enlightenment is a slow process that requires a lot of dedication and discipline. When we are born into this world, there is so much we have to learn. When you meet a loving Master whose purpose is only to help, heal and guide – a profound shift occurs. Everything seems different, sadness drifts away, and a loving energy takes its place.

You should be aware that every human being has a life plan and, although we do have free will, our destiny points will always be there. That we will meet those we have decided to meet; go through the problems and feel the pain we have chosen to feel. We also have debts to pay and dues to collect and if we do not deal with these correctly, we will have to re-live the same all over again. How we deal with all this depends on our free will. This is true of everyone; there are reasons for everything, and there are no exceptions.

It is only in the physical form that you must learn to feel pleasure and pain, for in the spiritual form there is no physical body and so this learning cannot be done. Therefore it is important that we do our best to get on with our learning in this world itself, as best we can. It is important to know yourself, to increase your understanding, and to practice loving kindness and detachment from worldly things. My writing has definitely helped me understand all this.

Baba says that in this period it is important to learn from our experience, for we always take our experiences with us. Baba also says that *'Real happiness lies in making others happy,'*[1] so do not hesitate to lend a helping hand. In order to become more aware of yourself, learn to overcome negative tendencies and help those who may need your help. Cast aside ego and pride. Be positive. Learn independence and freedom. Let go of anger and pride, practice forgiveness and faith, and, most of all, never, never be afraid. Know that Baba is always there to help you if you fall.

The key to our happiness lies in this life itself, and Baba's sincere advice to us is to live it to the fullest. Know that once we master our problem, it will never worry us again.

What then is Baba's answer to all this? It is Love – love that seeks only to give and asks nothing in return. Love helps us to cancel all our karmic debts and to get on the path to God and go towards the light. Karl once told me:

'Mum, I also have a dream – I dream that my Baba's name go far and wide – that the way He functions be publicised to the farthest corners of the world. I dream that all those who love Baba will always love Him wholeheartedly and completely – not because of what He can do for you – but because He is God.'

I have tried here to fulfil that dream.

And so we come to the end of another book. I have tried to fill the pages with truth, beauty, wisdom and a lot of love. The stories here are like flowers in a garden. After all, some people prefer roses; others love bluebells, orchids or lilies. Some choose pansies or sunflowers, while some just love the plain, green grass. They are all different but all of them are special. They all have one thing in common: Baba's Love Light shining on them to make them blossom, grow and look beautiful.

I thank all those who have had the courage to write their stories. I thank all those that have helped me in writing and producing this book; my family and friends for always standing beside me. Most of all, I thank my son Karl and, of course, my Beloved Meher Baba for coming into my life and enriching it so much with His love.

Meher Baba
A Biographical Note

Merwan Sheriar Irani was born in Pune, India, on February 25, 1894 at 5 am, to Zoroastrian parents of Persian descent. His father Sheriar, an ardent seeker of God, left his family at the age of twelve and began wandering through Iran in search of the Truth. For eight years, he led a penitent and ascetic life without any results. Frustrated and disappointed, he sailed for the port of Bombay. In India too, he wandered around with a staff and a bowl in his hands. His path crossed many sadhus and fakirs, and he took refuge at various places of pilgrimage. He only longed for the sight of his Beloved God – Yezdan. To achieve that, he went to the extent of undertaking *chilla-nashini*, a severe penance of forty days and nights, within a secluded circle, without food, water or sleep. After thirty days, unable to endure the torture a moment longer, he dragged himself away, collapsed near a river and fell into a deep slumber.

A Divine voice then spoke, "He whom you seek, He whom you wish to see, His attainment is not destined for you. Your son, it is your son who will attain it, and through your son – you."

Failing to achieve the enlightenment he sought, his steps eventually led him to Pune, to the home of his sister Piroja, who urged him to marry and settle down. Following his sister's advice, Sheriar married a girl in her early teens, Shireen Dorab Irani, who eventually bore him seven children.

Merwan was their second son and Sheriar knew that He was the one through whom his heart's longing would be fulfilled. A few early instances took place which confirmed his intuition.

In the early morning of the day Merwan was born, His mother Shireen saw a vision which she narrated to her mother.

"I saw a glorious person, like the sun sitting in a chariot, and His cool brilliance pervaded the atmosphere. A few people were pulling His chariot while thousands of people led Him in a procession. Tens of thousands of eyes were gazing at Him consoled by His Divine radiance."

A few months after Merwan was born, Shireen had a dream. She dreamt that she was standing at the doorway of their home, holding Merog (Merwan's affectionate family name) in her arms. Nearby was a well and out of it rose a beautiful Devi, like a Hindu goddess. She was dressed in a lavish green sari, her arms were covered from wrist to elbow with green glass bangles which tinkled as she held out her hands to Shireen and said, "Give me your Son; give Him to me." Frightened, Shireen held on to Merog all the more tightly and, awakened from her dream, was relieved to see Merog sleeping by her side.

As He grew, there were many such instances but, all in all, Merwan had an active and happy childhood. He was very alert, fast and mischievous. His friends called him "Electricity." He was kind and helped the poor and needy. He was a soft-hearted and mystical child with a deep interest in literature and poetry. He loved playing cricket, playing with marbles, flying kites, and listening to music. He was a good runner and a strong walker. He was a natural leader but never craved name or fame. He matriculated in 1911 from St. Vincent's High School, one of the finest in town, and later attended the Deccan College. However, His academic career came to an abrupt end in 1913 on a day that changed the entire course of His life.

Merwan used to cycle daily from His home to college and back. His daily route took Him past a neem tree under which sat Hazrat Babajan, a Muslim Perfect Master, around one hundred and twenty years of age. One day in May 1913, as Merwan passed by the tree, she suddenly looked at Him and beckoned. He got off His bicycle and walked over to her. He was drawn to her like steel to a magnet. Their eyes met. Babajan stood up and engulfed Him in her embrace with the fervour of a mother finding her lost son. Tears streamed down her wrinkled cheeks as she kept repeating, "Mera pyara beta..." my beloved son. Merwan was dazed. What He then experienced is indescribable – His individual consciousness was merged in the Ocean of Bliss. He walked home leaving His bicycle behind.

In due course, Merwan lost all interest in life. He was unable to concentrate on anything and could not express to anyone what He was experiencing. The only thing Merwan regularly did for the next seven months was to visit Babajan every day and sit by her side for long hours, sometimes late into the night. Then one fateful night in January 1914, just as Merwan was about to leave, He kissed Babajan's hand and she, in turn, held His face in her hands. The time had come. Babajan looked deeply into His eyes with all her love and kissed Him on the forehead. Turning to her followers gathered there she declared, "This is my Beloved Son. He will one day shake the world and all humanity will be benefited by Him." The Divinely ordained task of Babajan was accomplished. Merwan began experiencing the infinite bliss of *God-realisation*. In Baba's own words, given out later, *"At the time Babajan gave Me the nirvikalp experience of My own reality, the illusory physical, subtle and mental bodies – mind, worlds and one and all created things – ceased to exist for Me even as illusion. Then I began to see that only I, and nothing else, existed."* [1]

His mother, Shireen, worried endlessly as cruel neighbours jeered at Merwan's vacant looks. What had happened to her Merog? His father looked on with patience and sympathy at his young Son. He knew all along what was happening but did not speak. Merwan's eyes were open but they did not see. His ears were open but they did not hear. He was in the world, but not of it. He had gone somewhere far, far away. For the following nine months, He lived without sleep, staring vacantly into space. He never ate solid food and He grew gaunt and pale. If He sat, He would sit at one place for hours without moving. If He walked, He would continue doing it for hours until someone stopped Him. Much of His time would be spent sitting in solitude and total darkness in a tiny cubicle upstairs in the attic of His home.

In November 1914, Merwan started becoming somewhat normal and began recognising people and places around Him. He also started eating a very small quantity of food. He began singing Persian songs with deep fervour – He sang to the glory of God. He conversed with friends about God, the inner path, the need for a Guru, and other such spiritual subjects. The glow on His face became a halo, for He was absorbed in the highest state of spiritual consciousness.

Then He began visiting places of pilgrimage and saintly personages.

He visited Narayan Maharaj, the Perfect Master in Kedgaon. Darshan was on at his palace and Maharaj, wearing a gold crown, was seated on the silver throne of Dattatrey. Upon seeing Merwan, Maharaj stopped the darshan and had all the people disperse. He came down from his throne and taking Merwan by the hand, gently led Him to his throne where he made Him sit. Maharaj then removed a garland from his own neck and placed it around Merwan's and offered Him mango juice to drink. They talked for a while and then Merwan left the place. After this meeting, Merwan began to feel the glory of His Godhood.

Next, Merwan met another Perfect Master, Tajuddin Baba of Nagpur. Although Tajuddin was in a bad mood that day, not allowing anyone to come close to him, he became silent the moment he saw Merwan and walked towards Him with roses in his hands. Their eyes met and their gaze locked. Not a word was spoken. Tajuddin waved roses on Merwan's cheeks and forehead and, when Merwan turned to leave, he waved roses in a farewell gesture and muttered, "My rose, my heavenly rose!" Merwan had received His 'Taj' (Crown).

In the month of December 1915, He went to Shirdi to meet Sai Baba, the *Qutub-e-Irshad* – the head of the five Perfect Masters. As Sai Baba was returning from his *lendi* procession, Merwan stretched Himself full length on the ground in front of his feet. Paying obeisance to the young lad in return and in a deep resounding voice, Sai Baba uttered one majestic word, *Parvardigar*, meaning 'God the Almighty' – the Sustainer. In that instant, Sai Baba conferred Infinite Power upon Merwan.

Sai Baba then beckoned Merwan to walk down the road. There was an old Khandoba temple some three hundred yards away where Upasni Maharaj was living. When Merwan approached Maharaj with folded hands, Maharaj stood up and greeted Merwan, so to speak, with a stone, which he threw with such great force that it drew blood. It hit Merwan at the exact spot where Babajan had so lovingly kissed Him. That was the stroke of *Dnyan – Marefat of Haquiqat* or Divine Knowledge. With the force of this impact, Merwan's consciousness began returning to the gross world. But it took seven more years for Maharaj, who by now had shifted to Sakori, to help Merwan completely regain gross human consciousness.

The day finally arrived. The Avatar's Divine Mission was to begin. In January 1922, a few minutes before Merwan's departure from Sakori, Upasni Maharaj called Him into his hut and with folded hands proclaimed, "Merwan, You are *Adi Shakti* – the Primal Force! You are the Avatar and I salute You." Merwan wept tears of bliss and bowed down at the feet of the Perfect Master. For a long time, until the *tonga* went out of sight, Upasni Maharaj gazed as the dust stirred on the road. As Merwan departed from the 'King of the Yogis' to begin His mission, silent tears caressed the Sadguru's cheeks. They were tears of joy. And so at age twenty-seven, Merwan, young, strong and handsome, began His work for mankind.

Drawn by His Divinity and magnetic personality, a small group of men started collecting around Him and this formed the nucleus of His Mandali. One among them started addressing Him as Meher Baba, meaning the 'compassionate father'. Baba was most loving, but He was also a very strict disciplinarian. He emphasised love for God and selfless service as the twin divine qualities to annihilate the false separative ego. His motto was 'Mastery In Servitude'. His lovers are from all walks of life and from every community. He allowed each one to follow his or her own religion, but emphasised the need to understand and live by the crux of it rather than cling to its crust embodied in rites, rituals, ceremonies and dogmas. As for Himself, He said, *"I belong to no religion. Every religion belongs to Me. My own personal religion is of My being the Ancient Infinite One and the religion I teach to all is love for God, which is the truth of all religions."*[2]

Meher Baba established a community near Arangaon village in the Ahmednagar District of Maharashtra, which is called Meherabad. It is this place that He chose as His final resting place up on a hill. He Himself supervised the construction of the tomb and spent many days and weeks, at intermittent periods, sitting inside its crypt in prayer and meditation, to send forth the vibrations that have since brought much happiness and comfort to so many. His Tomb-Shrine or Samadhi, as it is now called, has become a place of pilgrimage for His lovers and for seekers of God throughout the world.

In Meherabad, His work embraced a free school where spiritual training was stressed. He opened a free dispensary and hospital to give medical assistance as well as shelter and food to the poor.

He inaugurated ashrams for the mad and the mast. A unique characteristic feature of Baba's activities in Meherabad, as well as at other places, was the manner in which He would suddenly and without any warning or any cogent reason stop a project midway regardless of time, money, energy spent on it, and regardless of its success. Baba considered all such external activities and projects as a mere scaffolding for His inner spiritual work. Just as the scaffolding is brought down once the building is constructed, Baba disbanded His external activities once His inner work was accomplished.

From July 10, 1925, Meher Baba began observing silence. This was not undertaken as a sort of penance. Baba says, *"My outward silence is no spiritual exercise. It has been undertaken and maintained solely for the good of others."*[3] He communicated initially by pointing at the letters and figures on the English alphabet board, which also He discontinued from October 7, 1954. Later on, He communicated by means of His unique hand gestures and facial expressions which His Mandali members were quite adept at interpreting. Through His Silence, He dictated several books and messages; chief among them are *Discourses* and *God Speaks*. He had given up writing from January 1, 1927 and also stopped touching money, except when distributing it to the poor.

Meher Baba worked extensively with what He termed as masts. Masts are spiritually advanced souls intoxicated in their intense love and longing for God. They are so absorbed in their direct awareness of God that they have lost consciousness of their physical bodies, actions and surroundings. Baba regarded these meetings with the masts as most crucial to His work on the earth plane – *"I work for the masts, and knowingly or unknowingly, they work for Me."*[4]

On the 16th of October 1949, Baba, together with selected companions – sixteen men and four women – embarked upon what He termed as the "New Life" – a life of absolute purity, a total lack of desire, a complete reliance on God, of remaining cheerful under all circumstances, and giving no importance to rites, rituals and ceremonies. During this phase, Baba bulldozed individual barriers of temper, habit patterns, attachments, hopes, desires, longing, and security. The Master-disciple relationship was relinquished and Baba, as the Elder Brother to all His companions, exemplified the life of a true seeker.

Meher Baba travelled several times throughout the world to 'lay cables' for His spiritual work. On one of His visits to the West in 1952, He inaugurated the Meher Spiritual Centre in Myrtle Beach, South Carolina, USA. Baba referred to it as His home in the West. He also established a new Sufi Order, which is devoid of the *Shariat* – external rites, rituals, ceremonies, and He named it 'Sufism Reoriented'. It is based on love and longing for God and the eventual experiential Union. In His later visits in 1956 and 1958, Baba visited various places in Australia and established the 'Avatar's Abode' in Woombye, Queensland, Australia.

Baba underwent two, self-imposed, automobile accidents and suffered immensely without a single sound. These were foretold by Him as a necessary part of His Universal Spiritual Work of taking upon Himself the sufferings of the world.

In spite of His pain and discomfort, He continued His work with the poor. He spent many hours washing the feet of lepers and distributing grain, cloth and money to thousands of poor and destitute people. Suffering did not deter Him from His work of 'awakening' people and sowing the seed of His love in their heart. He opened the floodgate of His love through travelling to remote parts of India and giving His public darshan to tens of thousands of His lovers. After one such darshan programme, Baba remarked, *"When you see Me giving darshan and prasad to thousands of people, it is neither mechanical nor meaningless. These are the means by which My love flows to humanity."*[5]

The last years of His life were spent in strict seclusion. It was a time for complete absorption into inner universal spiritual work. On the evening of July 30, 1968, Baba declared, *"My work is done. It is completed one hundred percent to My satisfaction..."*[6] Later on, Baba said, *"I have been saying: the Time is near, it is fast approaching, it is close at hand. Today I say: The Time has come. Remember this!"*[7]

On Friday, the 31st of January 1969, Meher Baba dropped His physical form at His residence at Meherazad at 12.15 pm. All those who sincerely love Him and have faith in Him can always feel His presence and His love. Thousands congregate at His Samadhi on that day which is called Amartithi, to perpetuate the memory of the Eternal Beloved. His tombstone reads – **"I HAVE COME NOT TO TEACH BUT TO AWAKEN."**

Meher Baba's approach to spiritual development transcends differences between the various factions of religious philosophy. He never sought to form a sect or proclaim a dogma. He attracted and welcomed people of all faiths and every social class. And so His lovers, without establishing any cult, or religion, continue to gather to discuss and read His works and express their reflections on His life and message through music, poetry, dance, drama, painting and other forms of art.

"I am nearer to you than your own breath. Remember Me and I am with you and My love will guide you."[8]

Avatar Meher Baba ki Jai!

Information for Pilgrims
to Meherabad

MEHERABAD

Meher Baba's Tomb-Shrine (Samadhi) situated in Upper Meherabad is open for darshan throughout the year from 6.30 am to 8.00 pm. Prayer and aarti are performed every day at 7.00 am and 7.00 pm.

Accommodations for the pilgrims, separate for men and women, are given at the Meher Pilgrim Retreat (MPR) at Upper Meherabad, the Dharamshala and the Hostels at Lower Meherabad. Accommodation is available from 15th June to 15th March each year. Prior reservation is necessary. With the opening of the new Meher Pilgrim Retreat in June 2006, the old Meher Pilgrim Centre (MPC) now functions as a Pilgrim Registration Centre and meeting hall.

The only place to stay open during summer months is the Andhra Rest House, Contact: Y. S. Rao, Tel: +91 9848111671, 0241 2548544.

MEHERAZAD

Home of Meher Baba where He lived with some of His Mandali. It continues to be the private residence of the Mandali members. It is open for pilgrims on Tuesdays, Thursdays and Sundays, during the posted timings.

RESERVATIONS AND CHECK-IN

Request for reservations in Meher Pilgrim Retreat (MPR) should contain full name of each person, date of birth, mailing/email address, phone numbers, date and time of arrival/departure.

For Meher Pilgrim Retreat, send to: pimco@mail.ambppct.org

Pilgrim Reservation, Avatar Meher Baba Trust, P.O. Bag 31, King's Road, Ahmednagar 414 001, Maharashtra, India.

Reservations can be confirmed maximum 6 weeks in advance. Telephone reservations are not accepted, but the office can be phoned to check on status, make changes, etc. Tel: 0241 2548733, 0241 2548736.

Check-in at Meher Pilgrim Retreat is available between the hours 10:00 am to 7:00 pm.

HOW TO GET TO MEHERABAD

From anywhere in India: Meherabad is outside Ahmednagar, Maharashtra State, and is accessible by rail and road from various parts of the country. The nearest airports are at Pune and Aurangabad, both about 2.5 hours away by road. Once you reach Ahmednagar Railway Station or the Bus Depot, you could cover the 6 kms distance to Meherabad by auto rickshaw or by local transport going towards Arangaon village.

From Mumbai (Bombay): By train, state transport buses or private coaches or taxis. By road, Mumbai-Meherabad distance is around 300 kms and can be covered in about 5 hours using the express highway and the Chalkan bypass, without entering Pune.

From Pune (Poona): By train, state transport buses, private coaches or taxis. Pune-Meherabad distance is around 100 kms and can be covered in 2.5 hours.

The Pilgrim Reservation Office provides information and help regarding travelling, and may also arrange for private pick-up from airports at Mumbai and Pune.

From MPC to MPR.
Left on Main Road (0.3 km)
Right to 1st Road. Follow around curves, parallel tracks to RR crossing. Right across tracks. Right 0.2 km to
1st road, take Left ... go straight.

Follow over bund. At top of hill, road goes right. Keep to the right. Continue on the curvy road until the MPR is on your right.

Distances:
MPC to Garden Condo turnoff 2.0 km
MPC to Stone Terrace 2.6 km
MPC to Bus entry sign 3.0 km
MPC to MPR parking/staff entry 3.2 km

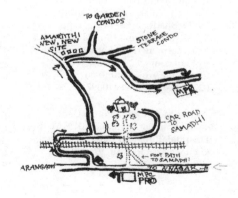

Centres of Information
about Meher Baba

INDIA

Avatar Meher Baba Perpetual Public
Charitable Trust,
P.O. Bag 31, King's Road,
Ahmednagar-414 001, Maharashtra.
Contact for Trust matters:
Mehernath Kalchuri.
Tel: 0241 2343666/7419/7093

Reservations at
Meher Pilgrim Retreat (MPR):
Contacts: Pat, Irene, Meredith.
Tel: 0241 2548733/36

Meher Pilgrim Retreat
Contacts: Heather Nadel, Adair,
Suzy. Tel: 0241 2548211

Avatar Meher Baba Bombay Centre,
Navyug Nivas, 'A' Block, 3rd flr.,
Dr. D. Bhadkamkar Marg, Opp.
Minerva Theatre, Mumbai 400 007.
E: avatarmeherbababombaycentre
@gmail.com
Contact: Cyrus Khambata
022 9987466878, 9821009715

Avatar Meher Baba Poona Centre,
441/1, Somwar Peth, Near K.E.M.
Hospital, Pune 411 011.
Contact: Pratap Ahir, 9763701780

Avatar Meher Baba Delhi Centre,
50A, Tughlakhabad Industrial Area,
M.B. Road, Near Batra Hospital,
New Delhi 110 062.
Contact: Manoj Sethi, 9810123853
Kusum Singh, 9313879011

Avatar Meher Baba Hyderabad
Centre, Esamia Bazar, Koti,
Hyderabad 500 027,
Andhra Pradesh.
Contact: Balaji, 9849090417

Avatar Meher Baba Centre
Meherpuri,
Hamirpur 201 301, U.P.
Contact: Pratap Chandra Nigam,
9450643629

Avatar Meher Baba
Tamil Nadu Centre,
22, Moorthy Nagar, Villivakkam,
Chennai 600 049.
Contact: Dinesh, 9840032490

Avatar Meher Baba Surat Centre,
B-3, Meher Prasad,
City Light, Parle Point,
Surat 395 007, Gujarat.
Contact: Rajnikant A. Mistry,
9601003886, 0261-2257555

OVERSEAS

Meher Spiritual Centre On The Lake,
10200 Highway 17, North Myrtle
Beach, South Carolina 29577, USA.

Meher Baba Foundation Australia,
P.O.B. 22, Woomby, Queensland
4559, Australia.

Sufism Reoriented Inc.,
1300 Boulevard Way, Walnut Creek,
California 94595, USA.

Meher Baba Information,
Anthony Thorpe, 3 Flowers Track,
Christchurch 8, New Zealand.

Avatar Meher Baba Centre of
Southern California,
1214 South Van Ness Avenue,
Los Angeles CA 90019-3520, USA.

SOME WEBSITES

avatarmeherbaba.in
avatarmeherbabatrust.org
avatarmeherbaba.org
meherbaba.com
meherabode.org
jaibaba.com
lovestreetbookstore.com

Meher Baba Association,
1/228 Hammersmith Grove,
London W6 7HG, England, UK.

For a detailed list, please visit: www.trustmeher.com/files/centers.htm

Patrick San Francisco

Patrick is based in Goa and hundreds flock to him every day in the hope that he will cure their various ailments. You may say it is desperation, but only those who have really suffered will understand the need that drives them to take this route for relief from suffering. How does one account for this? Yes, healing is a mystery and, even though a lot of people have been cured, it still remains a mystery.

Who or what guides Patrick?

At the early age of seventeen, an accident left him paralysed. The leading neuro-physicians came to his house to cure but they soon gave up on him. Well, what happened then? Young Patrick decided to stand up for himself. He told his family to close the door of his room and leave him alone for a while. He said to God, 'If you made me, you have to fix me.' And he had no doubt that it would work.

After a few days, Patrick went and opened the door.

That is how he got the confidence to start healing other people in a similar manner. That is why he now travels all over the world healing people of their pain and discomfort, emotional and mental problems, physical disabilities, their insecurities; even with problems in their love life. He does not heal through anyone or anything, but uses the earth's powerful positive energy to do his work for him. He harnesses the universal force around him and within him. It is all about the flow of energy and he believes implicitly in what he is doing with a total, unshakeable faith. This kind of faith that believes, without the smallest shred of doubt, is so hard to find. And when it does exist, it can produce, what we call, miracles.

Patrick conducting a healing session.

Patrick believes that God is the Ocean of Love. He says, 'A drop of water merges with the ocean ... God is the ocean, the drop is not.' He does not merely ask God for help – he demands it!

In this particular workshop, Patrick took great care to explain that the mantra he practices in order to heal is, 'The softness of kindness, the calmness of peace, and the warmth of love.' And it works for everyone. Healing for Patrick has now become a way of life. He is a pure and beautiful channel that allows the universal energy to flow through him and do its powerful healing.

Since he started healing, Patrick has also studied medicine and I was surprised to see some of the diagrams he drew. He appears to know all about the anatomy of the human body – how each organ should function and each nerve should respond.

He welcomes everyone with a smiling face. He works for under-privileged children and old peoples' homes, visits hospitals, and is kind to the poor. I find him to be an extremely gentle and humane person, one who is always ready to help and do his best to heal. I even took my dog Ruffles to him for healing. This is possibly because he only works with love and believes in finding the good in everyone. Unconditional love is one of the most difficult tests we humans have to pass, and once we manage to love people as they are without criticising or judging them, it becomes so much easier to be in touch with one's higher Self. I have no doubt that Patrick must be very high on the ladder leading to unconditional love!

How he manages to do it all; how he travels almost every single day from his home in Goa to far away Mumbai, Pune, Bangalore, Chandigarh, New Delhi, Chennai, Kolkata, Bijapur, Leh, and now even to Dubai, I really do not know!

Glossary

Aarti A traditional Hindu way of devotion and worship to God. A song or prayer with a refrain or theme which expresses the yearning for the offering of one's self to the One worshipped, or a song sung in God's praise describing His divine attributes and seeking His blessings.

Adi Shakti The active manifest power that creates the universe.

Agiary Parsi fire temple. A temple in which Parsis revere fire which is kept in a vessel called the afurganyu. The original ash, alat (implements for religious rituals), were brought from Iran in the 10th century to maintain the ritual continuity.

Ahuramazda The only God of the Zoroastrians, the Lord of Wisdom, helped by the seven attendant deities or the Amesha Spentas.

Amartithi Immortal Date. The day when Baba dropped His physical body – 31st January 1969.

Ashram A simple, humble, unostentatious abode of a spiritual teacher.

Auto writing An occult phenomenon where the writing is inspired by a spirit source other than the self.

Avatar The total manifestation of God in human form on earth; descent of God; also called the God-Man, the Messiah, the Buddha, the Christ, the Saviour, the Rasool, the Saheb-e-Zaman.

Avatar Meher Baba Ki Jai! Victory to. Used in the sense of 'Hail to.' 'Jai' in a greeting is used in the sense of calling upon the name of the Avatar, or in remembrance of the Avatar.

Bhajan-kirtan A bhajan is any type of Indian devotional song. It has no fixed form; it may be as simple as a mantra. Kirtan is call-and-response chanting performed in India's devotional traditions.

Bhakt Devotee, disciple.

Chilla-nashini Spiritual practice of penance and solitude, known mostly in Indian and Persian folklore. In this ritual, a mendicant or ascetic attempts to remain seated in a circle without food, water, or sleep for forty days and nights.

Daaman The hem of a garment. When Baba says, 'Hold on to My daaman,' it connotes love, obedience and surrender to Him.

Darbar Audience chamber.

Darshan An audience with the Master. An act of seeing, folding of hands in adoration or bowing at the feet of one's Master to express devotion. The spiritual presence of the Master at His Samadhi.

Dhuni A ceremonial fire lit on special occasions. As per Baba's wish, the dhuni is lit on the 12th of every month at Meherabad.

Diyas Oil lamps made of either clay or metal.

Dnyan Gnosis, knowledge of spiritual truths. In Sufism it is called Irfan.

Fakir Muslim Sufi ascetics or wandering Dervishes teaching Islam and living on alms.

God-realisation The goal of every spiritual seeker is to realise his own Divine Self, which is One within all and which is completely manifested in the Perfect Master.

Gurus A teacher. Generally referred to as a spiritual preceptor or Master.

Hara Osho wrote a note titled 'Hara Centering': The hara pumps life energy in and sends out clean, fresh chi energy to all parts of the body.

Hungama Noisy and boisterous clamour – a ruckus.

Jai Baba See Avatar Meher Baba Ki Jai!

Jhopdi A small hut usually made of mud and a thatched straw roof. Baba's Jhopdi is the place where He started His Silence, and never spoke again for the rest of His life.

Kabutarkhanas Places where pigeons are fed in.

Kalyug The fourth stage of the world's development that we are currently in. According to Hindu Scriptures, this is the age of rampant vice and corruption, and this stage will end on a final judgement day.

Karma Action. Also, the working of the law of action and reaction – effect, fate. The natural and necessary happenings of one's lifetime, preconditioned by one's past lives and actions in this life.

Karma yogi One who follows the path of selfless action and selfless service.

Lendi A ceremony in which Sai Baba of Shirdi would be taken in a procession with pomp and adoration to defecate every day at a fixed time. Sai Baba explained, 'When I pass my stool, I direct my 'abdals' – spiritual agents on the inner planes – about their duties to the world. I call upon them through the sound of the music during the parade.'

Mandali Close ones; used to describe Baba's close disciples.

Marefat of Haquiqat Divine knowledge.

Mast A God-intoxicated person on the spiritual path.

Mithai Indian sweets.

Nakshatra The term Nakshatra means Sky Map – 'naks' meaning 'sky' and 'shetra' meaning 'region'. The Nakshatras are like zodiacal signs except for the fact that they are more specific. Each Nakshatra has a mythological god whose duty it is to guard and guide the cosmic evolution.

Naseeb Fate.

Nazar To see. The Master's protective watch over His disciples.

Nirvikalp The experience of the "I am God" state of the Perfect Ones.

Occult Beyond the range of ordinary knowledge; mysterious. Not apparent on mere inspection, but discoverable by experimentation; the supernatural or supernatural agencies and affairs.

Paramatma The eternal supreme God.

Parsi Ethnically of Persian origin, with an ancestry that can be traced to the province of Khorasan known in ancient times as Parthia. Forced to leave Persia (Iran) because of persecution, the Parsis arrived on mainland India in 936 A.D. Followers of the Zoroastrian religion.

Parvardigar Vishnu. The Preserver or Sustainer.

Perfect Master A God-realised soul who retains God-consciousness and creation-consciousness simultaneously, and who has a duty in creation to help other souls towards the realisation of God. Also known as Qutub, Man-God or Sadguru.

Prasad A gift, usually edible, given by the Master which is symbolic of the inner spiritual gift that it conveys.

Puja Ritual worship of Hindu gods and goddesses performed with lighting of lamps and chanting of mantras and bhajans.

Reiki Universal energy. An ancient touch-healing system through the laying of hands.

Sadguru Perfect Master, Qutub, Man-God.

Sadhaks Followers or disciples of a spiritual master or teacher.

Sadhanas Spiritual practices involving meditation.

Sadra A shirt of very fine muslin.

Sahavas Intimate companionship. A gathering held by the Master or in His honour where the lovers and followers intimately feel His physical or spiritual presence.

Sahavasis Followers of Meher Baba.

Samadhi The tomb-shrine of a spiritual master. Meher Baba's Samadhi is at Meherabad, Ahmednagar, Maharashtra, India.

Sanskaras Accumulated imprints of past experiences which determine one's desires and actions in one's present life.

Sanyas Renunciation.

Sanyasis/sanyasins Male/female renunciates.

Sari A traditional female Indian garment of around five to six metres in length wrapped around the body.

Shariat The esoteric path, orthodoxy, external conformity to religious injunctions and traditions.

Spirit world A realm of imagination, where departed souls reside as spirits without gross bodies.

Sufis A mystic discipline whose origins are lost in antiquity. It is known to have existed at the time of Zoroaster, who is Himself said to be a Sufi. It is an expression of the way of life in which the goal is to purge the heart of everything but God through spiritual contemplation and ecstasy and to eventually achieve total absorption in God. It was revitalised by various Avatars. Adherents of the esoteric teachings of Prophet Muhammad came to be called Sufis. Sufism Reoriented, which is functioning in the West, follows Baba's Charter.

Surrender The self-surrender of a disciple whose wholehearted devotion to the Master opens himself for receiving the Divine Love which the Master pours on him. The disciple offers his life to the Master without reservation; his weaknesses as well as his strengths, his virtues as well as his vices, his merits as well as his sins. Until God-realisation, the faith that the disciple places in the Master is his guide.

Swami Title used to address a God-realised person of one of the several monastic orders who practices renunciation, celibacy, and asceticism, and who represents spiritual authority.

Taqdeer Destiny.

Tonga A horse-carriage used for transporting people.

Udhi The ash from Dhuni – the sacred fire.

Yantras An abstract geometric pattern drawn on paper or etched on metal plate, signifying the unique characteristics of a deity or group of deities.

Zoroastrian A system of thought, feeling and action which is shared by the followers of Zarathustra the Prophet.

Source Notes and Copyright Details

Chapter 9 – The Pilgrim's Progress

[1] *Life At Its Best,* Copyright © 1957 by Sufism Reoriented Inc. San Francisco, California.

Chapter 11 – All Are One

[1] *Lord Meher,* Copyright Bhau Kalchuri. Original Hindi edition © 1973, English translation © 1973, both by Bhau Kalchuri. English translation edited by Lawrence Reiter. Used with author's permission, Vol. 13, p. 4421.

Chapter 13 – From Art to Heart

[1] *Lord Meher,* Copyright Bhau Kalchuri. Original Hindi edition © 1973, English translation © 1973, both by Bhau Kalchuri. English translation edited by Lawrence Reiter. Used with author's permission, Vol. 20, p. 6533.

[2] *Lord Meher,* Copyright Bhau Kalchuri. Original Hindi edition © 1973, English translation © 1973, both by Bhau Kalchuri. English translation edited by Lawrence Reiter. Used with author's permission, Vol. 5, p. 1656-58.

Chapter 14 – Baba's Silence

[1] *Universal Message,* Meherabad, July 10, 1958, Copyright Avatar Meher Baba Perpetual Public Charitable Trust, Ahmednagar, India.

[2] *Universal Message,* Meherabad, July 10, 1958, Copyright Avatar Meher Baba Perpetual Public Charitable Trust, Ahmednagar, India.

[3] *Lord Meher,* Copyright Bhau Kalchuri. Original Hindi edition © 1973, English translation © 1973, both by Bhau Kalchuri. English translation edited by Lawrence Reiter. Used with author's permission, Vol. 2, p. 735.

[4] *Lord Meher,* Copyright Bhau Kalchuri. Original Hindi edition © 1973, English translation © 1973, both by Bhau Kalchuri. English translation edited by Lawrence Reiter. Used with author's permission, Vol. 2, p. 737.

[5] *Lord Meher,* Copyright Bhau Kalchuri. Original Hindi edition © 1973, English translation © 1973, both by Bhau Kalchuri. English translation edited by Lawrence Reiter. Used with author's permission, Vol. 2, p. 737.

[6] *Lord Meher,* Copyright Bhau Kalchuri. Original Hindi edition © 1973, English translation © 1973, both by Bhau Kalchuri. English translation edited by Lawrence Reiter. Used with author's permission, Vol. 16, p. 5606.

[7] *Lord Meher,* Copyright Bhau Kalchuri. Original Hindi edition © 1973, English translation © 1973, both by Bhau Kalchuri. English translation edited by Lawrence Reiter. Used with author's permission, Vol. 19, p. 6347.

[8] *Lord Meher,* Copyright Bhau Kalchuri. Original Hindi edition © 1973, English translation © 1973, both by Bhau Kalchuri. English translation edited by Lawrence Reiter. Used with author's permission, Vol. 19, p. 6347.

[9] *Lord Meher,* Copyright Bhau Kalchuri. Original Hindi edition © 1973, English translation © 1973, both by Bhau Kalchuri. English translation edited by Lawrence Reiter. Used with author's permission, Vol. 13, p. 4424.

[10] *Lord Meher,* Copyright Bhau Kalchuri. Original Hindi edition © 1973, English translation © 1973, both by Bhau Kalchuri. English translation edited by Lawrence Reiter. Used with author's permission, Vol. 16, p. 5486.

[11] *The Silent Master,* © 1967, Meher Baba Archives.

Chapter 16 – Writings on the Wall

[1] *Lord Meher,* Copyright Bhau Kalchuri. Original Hindi edition © 1973, English translation © 1973, both by Bhau Kalchuri. English translation edited by Lawrence Reiter. Used with author's permission, Vol. 16, p. 5487.

Chapter 17 – The Pune Circle

[1] *Discourses*, Meher Baba, 7th ed., p. 3, Copyright Avatar Meher Baba Perpetual Public Charitable Trust, Ahmednagar, India.

[2] *Lord Meher*, Copyright Bhau Kalchuri. Original Hindi edition © 1973, English translation © 1973, both by Bhau Kalchuri. English translation edited by Lawrence Reiter. Used with author's permission, Vol. 12, pp. 4217-4218.

[3] *Lord Meher*, Copyright Bhau Kalchuri. Original Hindi edition © 1973, English translation © 1973, both by Bhau Kalchuri. English translation edited by Lawrence Reiter. Used with author's permission, Vol. 8, p. 2874.

[4] *Lord Meher*, Copyright Bhau Kalchuri. Original Hindi edition © 1973, English translation © 1973, both by Bhau Kalchuri. English translation edited by Lawrence Reiter. Used with author's permission, Vol. 8, p. 2995.

[5] *Discourses*, Meher Baba, 7th ed., pp. 380 – 381, Copyright Avatar Meher Baba Perpetual Public Charitable Trust, Ahmednagar, India.

Chapter 18 – Hold On

[1] *Lord Meher*, Copyright Bhau Kalchuri. Original Hindi edition © 1973, English translation © 1973, both by Bhau Kalchuri. English translation edited by Lawrence Reiter. Used with author's permission, Vol. 12, p. 4219.

[2] *Lord Meher*, Copyright Bhau Kalchuri. Original Hindi edition © 1973, English translation © 1973, both by Bhau Kalchuri. English translation edited by Lawrence Reiter. Used with author's permission, Vol.13, p. 4624.

Chapter 19 – Reaching Beyond

[1] *Lord Meher*, Copyright Bhau Kalchuri. Original Hindi edition © 1973, English translation © 1973, both by Bhau Kalchuri. English translation edited by Lawrence Reiter. Used with author's permission, Vol. 8, p. 2993.

Conclusion

[1] *Lord Meher*, Copyright Bhau Kalchuri. Original Hindi edition © 1973, English translation © 1973, both by Bhau Kalchuri. English translation edited by Lawrence Reiter. Used with author's permission, Vol. 15, p. 5262.

Meher Baba – A Biographical Note

[1] *Listen, Humanity*, Meher Baba, narrated and edited by D. E. Stevens, 1957 © Avatar Meher Baba Perpetual Public Charitable Trust, Ahmednagar, Appendix II, p. 245.

[2] *Lord Meher*, Copyright © Bhau Kalchuri, author in Hindi, English translation by Lawrence Reiter, Vol. 12, p. 4341.

[3] *Lord Meher*, Copyright © Bhau Kalchuri, author in Hindi, English translation by Lawrence Reiter, Vol. 12, p. 6533.

[4] *The Silent Master*, Copyright © Meher Baba Archives, 1967, p. 36.

[5] *Lord Meher*, Copyright © Bhau Kalchuri, author in Hindi, English translation by Lawrence Reiter, Vol. 11, p. 4062.

[6] *Lord Meher*, Copyright © Bhau Kalchuri, author in Hindi, English translation by Lawrence Reiter, Vol. 20, p. 6641.

[7] *Last Sahavas*, Copyright © Dr. H. P. Bharucha.

[8] *Meher Baba Calling*, p. 29. Copyright © Avatar Meher Baba Perpetual Public Charitable Trust, Ahmednagar.

Photo Credits

Chapter 1, p. 3, Meher Baba in a wheelchair after his accident at Satara, March, 1957, MSI Collection.

Chapter 12, p. 115, Meher Baba, Homyar J. Mistry, Homz Prints.

Chapter 14, p. 131, Meher Baba's Jhopdi, Soumya C. Khambata.

Chapter 16, p. 148, Writings On The Wall, MPR, Homyar J. Mistry, Homz Prints.

Chapter 16, p. 153, Divine Beloved, Soumya C. Khambata.

Chapter 18, p. 163, Cover page of *God-Brother – Stories from my Childhood with Meher Baba*, by Mani S. Irani, Copyright © Avatar Meher Baba Perpetual Public Charitable Trust, Ahmednagar. Illustrated by Wodin.

Appendix A, p. 189, Avatar Meher Baba ki Jai!, Copyright © Avatar Meher Baba Perpetual Public Charitable Trust, Ahmednagar.

Recommended Reading

The following books on Meher Baba are available at Avatar Meher Baba Perpetual Public Charitable Trust, Ahmednagar, and the Bombay Centre, Navyug Nivas, Bhadkamkar Marg, A-wing, 3rd floor, Mumbai 400 007. Also available are brooches, lockets, audio CDs, VCDs/DVDs.

Avatar, *Jean Adriel*
Beams from Meher Baba on the Spiritual Panorama, *Meher Baba*
Conversations with the Awakener (Series), *Bal Natu*
Discourses, *Meher Baba*
Glimpses of the God-Man Vol. 1 to 6, *Bal Natu*
God Brother, *Manija S. Irani*
God Speaks, *Meher Baba*
How a Master Works, *Ivy O Duce*
In God's Hand, *Meher Baba*
Life at its Best, *Meher Baba*
Listen, Humanity Meher Baba, *Don Stevens*
Lord Meher, *Bhau Kalchuri*
Meher Baba The Awakener of the Age, *Don Stevens*
Mehera, *Compiled by Janet Judson*
Mehera-Meher, *David Fenster* (out of print)
Much Silence, *Tom & Dorothy Hopkinson*
Path of Love, *Meher Baba*
Sparks of the Truth from the dissertations of Meher Baba, *Dr. C.D. Deshmukh*
Stay with God, *Francis Brabazon*
That's How It Was, *Eruch Jessawala*
The Beloved, *Naosherwan Anzar*
The Everything and the Nothing, *Meher Baba*
The Samadhi: Star of Infinity, *Bal Natu*
Wayfarers, *William Donkin* (out of print)

The author may be contacted on email:
umrigar@vsnl.com

For further details, contact:
Yogi Impressions Books Pvt. Ltd.
1711, Centre 1, World Trade Centre,
Cuffe Parade, Mumbai 400 005, India.

Fill in the Mailing List form on our website
and receive, via email, information on
books, authors, events and more.
Visit: www.yogiimpressions.com

Telephone: (022) 61541500, 61541541
Fax: (022) 61541542
E-mail: yogi@yogiimpressions.com

 Join us on Facebook:
www.facebook.com/yogiimpressions

Sounds Of Silence

A Bridge Across Two Worlds

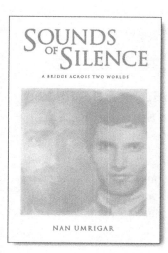

NAN UMRIGAR

"Mummy, my dearest Mummy, I love you so much more than you can imagine on earth. On earth I never realised I loved you so much. Please Mummy, forget the past, for now I am very happy..."

– Karl's first words, from the afterlife, to his mother Nan.

"I had absolutely no leanings towards spirituality or spiritualism for that matter," says Nan Umrigar. "But all of this changed with the death of my son Karl, a champion jockey, whose accident on the race track of Mumbai cut short a brilliant career. My grieving family questioned the unjust hand of fate, and nothing could fill the void, till the time I met some people who communicated with their loved ones from the spirit world."

Soon, Nan also began communicating with her son and received messages that were to change her life forever. Sounds came in from the silence – conquering the great divide and proving that there is something far beyond the life we live. *Sounds of Silence* traces in moving detail her joy at coming in touch with Karl once again, and her gradual introduction to Meher Baba, her son's guru in the afterlife.

In *Sounds of Silence* Nan bares her soul, reflecting her own initial scepticism and doubts, until the weight of the evidence left her in no doubt about the reality of the messages. This is a book that challenges many concepts about life and death and particularly life after death.

Originally self-published, *Sounds of Silence* fast became an 'underground' bestseller, and a tremendous source of strength for thousands who were drawn to it. This is a story of a mother's unrelenting hope, and of a love that never dies.

LISTENING
TO THE SILENCE

TRUE STORIES OF A HEALING LOVE FROM THE SPIRITUAL REALMS

NAN UMRIGAR
AUTHOR OF 'SOUNDS OF SILENCE'

Listening
To The Silence

True stories of a Healing Love from the Spiritual Realms

"There will be many people who will call on you for help... once they come to Him, He takes care of them... All you have to do is bring them to Him."

– Karl

Nan's story that began with her best-selling book, *Sounds of Silence*, reached out to touch hearts all across the world. Her journey that started alone has now been joined by countless others whose pain and sadness have been washed away, and their lives turned around, by the healing love of Meher Baba – a spiritual Master from the higher realms.

Her son Karl's loving and caring messages of hope from the spirit world inspire and stir the hearts, and strengthen the resolve of those who come forward to listen to the silence within and find their own answers – through the grace of the Master. Through these answers, Nan's own life begins to take on a deeper spiritual meaning.

Her story now moves compellingly forward, interwoven with a collection of personal, heart-touching narrations of the wondrous experiences people have had – when they have opened their hearts to the Master.

In *Listening to the Silence*, Nan shows how the Master works only and absolutely – through the power of love. She also shares with us her deeper understanding of the evolution of consciousness, life and death, karma, compassion, love and forgiveness, and of the onward journey of the soul.

More importantly, *Listening to the Silence*, gives you the strength to triumph over adversity, to evolve your own path and lead a life of self-fulfillment.

Made in the USA
Las Vegas, NV
01 June 2023

72800195R00125